Seeds of
Abundance

Dr Nikki Krampah CNHP, ND

authorHOUSE®

AuthorHouse™
1663 Liberty Drive
Bloomington, IN 47403
www.authorhouse.com
Phone: 1 (800) 839-8640

Published by AuthorHouse 01/18/2016

ISBN: 978-1-5049-6989-5 (sc)
ISBN: 978-1-5049-6988-8 (hc)
ISBN: 978-1-5049-6987-1 (e)

Library of Congress Control Number: 2015921062

Preface

NEVER ESTIMATE THE POWER OF A TINY SEED. ALTHOUGH QUITE SMALL IT HAS THE POWER WITHIN IT TO TRANSFORM AND TRANSFER LIFE. ALL LIFE BEGINS WITH A SEED. WE REMAIN BOUNDLESS, UNATTACHED WHEN WE ALLOW OUR THOUGHTS TO COINCIDE WITH OUR ACTIONS. THE WHOLE INTENT AND PURPOSE OF WRITING THIS BOOK IS TO OPEN THE MINDS OF IT'S READERS TO A WORLD OF POSSIBILITIES. YOU ALSO WILL BECOME BETTER ACQUAINTED WITH YOURSELF AND YOUR PURPOSE IN LIFE. HOW TO LIVE A RICH ABUNDANT LIFE FILLED OF LOVE, PEACE AND HARMONY. WHICH WILL SPILL OVER INTO YOUR RELATIONSHIPS, BE IT FAMILY, FRIENDS OR YOUR MATE. FIRST GATHER YOURS SEEDS (YOUR THOUGHTS), PLANT THEM (IN THE SOIL OF YOUR MIND), THEN PREPARE FOR A GREAT HARVEST (THE REALITY OF WHAT YOU'VE SOWN). WITH TRUE DEFINITION AND PURPOSE DIRECT YOUR THOUGHTS AND START IMPLEMENTING THESE TINY LITTLE GEMS OF WISDOM INTO YOUR LIFE. MOST IMPORTANTLY BE READY TO RECEIVE, THEN BE OPEN TO GIVE WITHOUT REMORSE. THE MEASURE THAT YOU GIVE OUT, IS THE SAME MEASURE IN WHICH YOU SHALL RECEIVE. SOWINGS SEEDS OF ABUNDANCE IS NOT AS HARD AS MANY PERCEIVE. THE NATURAL ORDER OF THINGS ARE ALREADY SET IN MOTION. YOU DON'T HAVE TO WORK EXTREMELY HARD TO GET THE RETURN FROM THE FRUITS OF YOUR LABOR. HOWEVER YOU DO HAVE TO PLANT THEM. YOU HAVE TO BE WILLING TO TRANSFORM YOUR MIND AND SPIRIT AND DEBUNK YOUR MIND FROM ANYTHING THAT MAY BE A POTENTIAL THREAT TO YOUR PATH OF ABUNDANCE. IN OTHER WORDS, IF YOU HAVE NEGATIVE THOUGHTS AND YOU EXPECT GOOD THINGS TO HAPPEN THEN YOU ARE NOT THINKING IN HARMONY WITH THE LAW. WHATEVER SEEDS ARE SOWN GOOD OR BAD SHALL BE REAPED IN IT'S OWN KIND. THERE WILL BE PEOPLE THAT WILL COME TO TEST YOU ON YOUR

JOURNEY BUT REST ASSURE THAT THIS IS ALL APART OF THE PROCESS. LET IT HAPPEN THE WAY THAT IT SHOULD, DO NOT RESIST THE PROCESS. ALLOW FEEDBACK TO COME FROM OTHERS, THIS IS HOW WE GROW. FURTHERMORE ALL FEEDBACK IS NOT GOOD, SO DECIPHER WHAT IS VALID FROM INVALID INFORMATION. DO NOT SHARE WITH ANYONE WHAT YOU ARE DOING, YOU DON'T NEED THE CONSPIRACY OPINIONS. IN THIS MOMENT YOU ARE BEING RENEWED. TAKE TO HEED THAT THIS BOOK IS WORTHY OF YOUR UNDIVIDED ATTENTION. WITH THAT BEING SAID, DO NOT SHORT CHANGE YOUR PROGRESS OR YOURSELF. HENCEFORTH YOU WILL LEARN THE SECRETS TO SUCCESS AND HOW TO KEEP A DOWNPOUR OF ABUNDANCE FLOWING IN YOUR LIFE, ON COMPLETION OF READING THIS BOOK.

NIKKI KRAMPAH, ND

Dedication

THIS BOOK IS DEDICATED TO MY SOVEREIGN GOD JEHOVAH, UNIVERSAL CREATOR, HEALER AND GOD OF INFINITE WISDOM. BY HIS LOVE AND MERCY I WAS ABLE TO WRITE THIS BOOK ON WHAT I THOUGHT WAS MY DEATH BED. THROUGH MUCH COOPERATION AND OBEDIENCE, I WITNESSED MY OWN HEALING TAKING PLACE. I AM GRATEFUL FOR HIS TENDER MERCIES AND THANKFUL FOR COMING TO KNOW HIM MORE FULLY. TO MY MOTHER KIMBERLY WHO WAS SUCH A SOUND WOMAN SPIRITUALLY, FOR TEACHING ME THAT GOD IS REAL AND HEARS OUR CRIES FOR HELP AND HAS THE POWER TO HEAL US. SHE MADE HIM MORE REAL TO ME WITH THE AID OF THE BIBLE. TO MY WONDERFUL HUSBAND THAT GOD USED AS AN INSTRUMENT TO HELP HEAL ME BOTH FROM MRSA AND BREAST CANCER. WHO SUPPORTED ME NOT ONLY IN MY HEALING, BUT THE WRITING OF THIS BOOK AND MY CAREER AND GOALS, EVEN TO THE EXTENT OF PUTTING MY GOALS BEFORE HIM. TO MY CHILDREN FOR REMAINING SO SUPER AND BEING THE POSITIVE LIGHT THAT BRINGS ME JOY.

AND TO ALL OF MY FRIENDS WHO INSPIRED ME TO WRITE, THIS BOOK IS TO ALL OF MY LOVELIES. THANKS FOR YOUR SUPPORT AND BELIEVING IN ME. LAST AND CERTAINLY NOT LEAST DR CHUCK LANDON MY BEST FRIEND, I WILL NEVER FORGET YOU. YOU INSPIRED ME SO MUCH THAT IF GOD HAD NOT USED ME, I PROBABLY WOULD NOT HAVE SEEN MY FULLEST POTENTIAL. YOU HELPED ME TO SEE THAT THERE WAS MORE JOY IN GIVING THAN RECEIVING. I SAW ALL THE PEOPLE YOU HAD HELPED HEAL FROM VARIOUS DISEASES AND KNEW THAT THE WORK WAS GREAT INDEED. I NOW UNDERSTAND THAT GOD IS GREATER THAN OUR FEARS AND THAT HIM AND I TOGETHER ARE THE MAJORITY.

Sowing

Sowing

Consciousness creates form; and thought creates reality. The seeds that we sow start in our conscious thoughts. Once they have been accepted as true or false they are stored in the data-base we call our subconscious mind. Here, there is no more filtering, for the subconscious mind accepts everything that the conscious deems as true. It does not interject. From here it shapes the things in your life events, situations etc... starts to show up, out of the subconscious mind they are born into the physical realm.

Are you familiar with the phrase "You create your own reality," often referred to as the acronym, YCYOR! YCYOR is a powerful manifesto; one that most certainly gives pause for thought. And pause we should, if thought is truly the rainmaker of our physical reality and circumstances, that would mean that circumstances do not happen to us, but by us. Pretty interesting concept, isn't it?

Early on I had become quite enamored by such a prospect. Could it really be so that reality as we know it is but a construct of the human mind and do we have the ability to consciously shape our own reality? Whatever the case, would it not be of extreme importance to monitor what comes in or goes out of our most prized possession, our minds?

We sow our seeds first by our thoughts. What we think gives birth to our dreams, ambitions, ideas, desires and goals.

So many of us are used to functioning in "autopilot mode" that we really don't do much thinking at all. Acting only on impulse and only reacting off of emotional stimuli be it right or be it wrong. This is the same mode that will leave you in a relationship that you very well are aware of is unhealthy. However you are so comfortable with the routine of it all. Maybe your stuck in a dead end job that you know you're not being recognized for advancement, nor being considered for another position, that you more than qualify for, but you stay anyway because you know the job so well, you can do it in your sleep. The problem with both scenarios is you mind is not being challenged. Although both are stressful, which can be challenging, these situations are not pushing you to strive for what is better.

Another form of sowing is by our deeds, rather good or bad, we will meet the full recompense of them all and nothing can circumvent this.

Last but certainly not least are our words. Yes the bible says it better than I have ever heard said before. It says "Life and death are in the power of the tongue."

Since the mouth is referred to as being so powerful it can either build or destroy. This is one body member that will surely payoff in the long run if we train it properly and is worthy of getting the mastery over. If you think that your tongue is too small to make a difference, then try sleeping with an mosquito. Then you will see, that the size of an object doesn't matter. Pun intended.

One thing we ought to comprehend is that we sow seeds consistently either in our lives or in the lives of others. We sow seeds physically, inwardly, profoundly and rationally. In assuming that you plant negative seeds through negative musings you will have cynicism in your life in full bloom. Just like plants, you need to sustain your contemplations of thoughts and empower them to develop in a positive way so you can have a positive feedback in life. Each seed that we sow carries its own harvest either for great or for terrible. Our brain is the second strongest force to our soul. What we allow to enter has a powerful effect on the subconscious mind. It could be likened to a DVD, a Digital Versatile Disk, in which you can reprogram and wipe at anytime. For instance, when we do something kind for others, like providing for them a blessing, we are sowing seeds of gifts and bliss. When we say a kind word, we are sowing. seeds of adoration and certification.

When we petition God for others and ask God to meet their necessity or help them in an area that they are battling, we are sowing seeds of trust, leniency and beauty. No matter the crux of the situation or the nature of our problems. We seem to know from out of them we will be delivered

Dr Nikki Krampah CNHP, ND

and will soon taste beauty for ashes. When we recognize a deed well done or compliment somebody on a ability they have, we are sowing seeds of encouragement. As we keep sowing these tiny little seeds, remember that they will multiply and in due time we will yield a bountiful harvest.

Different Aspects of Thought

Different Aspects of Thought

When you think about it, even on the most fundamental level, before anything can materialize, it has to first originate in thought. For instance, you go to meet a friend for dinner. How did the reality of having dinner with a friend make its way to a physical event? First the thought enters your head. Initially, having dinner is an option. Then you imagine what the evening may be like: Great food, the ambiance, stimulating conversation etc. The thought begins to gain more momentum, which gives birth to imagination. Then you settle on the idea that you would indeed enjoy having dinner with your friend and so you proceed to take the physical steps to make it happen: a phone call to see if your friend is free for the evening, another call to make reservations at a favorite restaurant and of course the act of playing out the thought – dinner with a friend. Where did it all begin? In the mind of course. For if the event was not first planted in our mind it wouldn't have ability to play out.

Of course, this is a simplistic illustration of how thought creates reality and furthermore, we are speaking of conscious thought. There are other layers – more subtle layers that can be incredibly powerful in creating our reality. And in fact, this process may be the most potent form of reality creation.

"We are like 'Iceberg Beings' – Most of us is beneath the surface."

-Michael Talbot
(author of The Holographic Universe)

Sowing Seeds by Deeds

Sowing Seeds by Deeds

"With every deed you are sowing a seed, though the harvest you may not see."

-Ella Wheeler Wilcox

Each seed that we sow will fall into the soil of somebody's heart. It will flourish, develop and carry to realization what was planted by "us" the "sower." That is the reason why we must be cognizant to what we are stating and doing to others. We are either planting great seeds to favor, energize and fortify them or on the other hand we are planting awful seeds that will debilitate others and make them question their very own existence. Give ourselves a chance to recollect the force of our activities and be constant in lifting others up and revealing to them the correct significance that exists within their being.

An alternate range concerning the seed is providing for God monetarily. How would we provide for God? In the Old Testament all individuals were charged to give a tenth of what they had over to God and that might guarantee their continued favoring from Him. As New Testament Christians, we are not directed to give 10% of our pay, however we are advised to give to the extent that originates from our heart. We read in 2 Corinthians 9:7-8 "Each man to the extent that he purposes in his heart, so let him give; not grudgingly, or of need: for God loveth a joyful giver. What's more God has the capacity to make all effortlessness proliferate to you; that ye, continually having all sufficiency in all things, may proliferate to each great work." We are advised to give merrily and on the grounds that we do, God will make His beauty flourish towards us. (King James Version)

I move you to be a giver in life. Sow your seeds intentionally. Say kind words, do kind deeds, lift others up, and give from your entire heart so God may have the capacity to return it once more to you reproduced numerous times over. Where would it be advisable for you to give? Wherever it is required. Provide for your congregation, provide for the service that nourishes you profoundly, provide for the safe houses that help others, provide for the spots where you can see foods grown from the ground approaching from it, like local organic farmers. Provide for the place that is honored since that is great ground with great soil and will come back to you a great harvest.

The sublime thing about seeds is they duplicate significantly when planted in a fertile ground and the measure of harvest you appropriate is straightforwardly related to the measure of seeds that you've sown. The Biblical canon proclaims in 2 Corinthians 9:6 "However this I say, He which soweth sparingly might harvest likewise sparingly; furthermore he which soweth abundantly should procure additionally plentifully." A farmer doesn't have a go at searching for the harvest he never planted and it is the same with us. We shouldn't hope to harvest in spots where we've never planted. The point when we give merrily with an open heart, we can hope to gain the same in kind. A straightforward quote I adore says "Providers pick up". It may sound inverse to some, yet the supplier knows all excessively well how accurate it is. Be encouraged to attempt it for yourself and accept the gift of being a supplier. Continuously keep in mind the person who gives the most additionally increases the most.

Domingo's Story

God is Alive and Imparts Me With Strength

My name is Domingo and I would like to share my life changing story in hope that it could help other people going through hard times. I was exposed to Jehovah at a young age 9, but I wasn't quite knowledgeable yet, because I lived with an alcoholic father who beat me and raped me till I was 14. I ran away and hitch hiked to California where I lived for 4 years as a male prostitute, taking drugs and drinking. The whole time I was working the streets, I was running from life and God.

At the age of 18 I was arrested for prostitution and was sent home to my mothers house with a new step-father. I liked this new way of life and started going to my congregation again and tried to stay on the right path. Satan stepped in again to keep me working the streets, but still going to my meetings was in itself a battle with my own soul. I stayed in this situation till I was 25, stuck in limbo, then I went to jail for 6 months for prostitution. Here I was a manager at a local retail store and working the streets. The whole time I was a mess, always depressed and lonely looking for love. I did my time in jail and that's when I met a man that knew God, I studied the word of God for those 6 months and prayed for my soul. When I got out of jail I still lived with a male lover for 2 yrs. going on with life thinking that it was okay to do this. I was so ashamed, I would even hide him when I had my bible studies. I started to feel bad and no longer wanted to live like this.

At the age of 29, I met a women who was 10 years older, and had 5 children. I began dating her and ended up falling in love with her and giving up my gay lifestyle, or so I thought. In a year we were married and now I took on a family, and still the feelings for men were attacking me all the time. After several years of marriage and several affairs with men on the side I could not take it anymore. Here I was married to a wonderful woman and 5 adopted children; I often wondered why God sent me someone in whom I did not't deserve.

WHAT WAS I DOING? Since then I have dedicated my life to Jehovah along with my wife and have not looked back since! My conscience is now clean, I no longer desire to live a debauched lifestyle. What is of more significance, I long to help others. Putting my instant self gratifications on the back-burner. In helping others, I no longer feel that woe is me, self-pity. I am using my power to give to others as my fuel to keep me going and it has served me quite well.

One day my wife and I got up to go to work. We had been praying for months for the Lord to take over our lives and to be of more service, when this day I was driving an hour and half to work. I got off of the expressway at 7:30 am the same time my wife opened our door to a little girl who asked her for clothing, all she had on was rags. My wife gave her an outfit.

When I got off of the expressway, there was a man dirty and asking for food, I gave him my last $10.00 and told him across the street was a truck stop where he could take a clean up. Around the same time my wife shut the door and decided she wanted to see where the small girl was going. When she opened the door, the girl was gone, as I turned on the road I looked in my mirror to see that the man made it across the busy street and he was gone. When my wife and I saw each other after work we told each other our stories (Angels, no other answer).

No matter what our lot in life is, Jehovah can use us from where we are planted. In this story both husband and wife did a good deed at the same time. However, notice what this man has previously encountered. Being raped and molested by his own blood father, a life of prostitution and he struggled with addictions. Yet still God used him as a worthy vessel to bless someone else. Domingo did not allow life to make him bitter or so engrossed with pain, that he counted his soul dear to himself. Instead he asked Jehovah to willingly direct him and his wife and they chose to be of service to others. Today him and his wife owns a non-for-profit business taking care of the mis-fortunate, by providing food, clothing and shelter. What a wonderful story of sowing good seeds indeed.

Read and meditate on these scriptures:

Galatians 6:9-10 "And let us not be weary in well doing: for in due season we shall reap, if we faint not. As we have therefore opportunity, let us do good unto all men, especially unto them who are of the household of faith."

Galatians 6:7-8 "Be not deceived; God is not mocked: for whatsoever a man soweth, that shall he also reap. For he that soweth to his flesh shall of the flesh reap corruption; but he that soweth to the Spirit shall of the Spirit reap life everlasting."

Romans 12:19-21 "Dearly beloved, avenge not yourselves, but rather give place unto wrath: for it is written, Vengeance is mine; I will repay, saith the Lord. Therefore if thine enemy hunger, feed him; if he thirst, give him drink: for in so doing thou shalt heap coals of fire on his head. Be not overcome of evil, but overcome evil with good."

Proverbs 8:32-36 "Now therefore hearken unto Me, O ye children: for blessed are they that keep My ways. Hear instruction, and be wise, and refuse it not. Blessed is the man that heareth Me, watching daily at My gates, waiting at the posts of My doors. For whoso findeth Me findeth life, and shall obtain favour of the LORD. But he that sinneth against Me wrongeth his own soul: all they that hate Me love death."

Sowing Seeds by Words

Sowings Seeds by Word

"Weeping may stay for a night, but joy comes in the morning."

Psalm 30:5

Joy is a choice, it is a decision that you make that come what may, you are determined to stay in the "secret hiding place of Jehovah." In that place no one can steal your joy, because joy abounds all around you. Look up in the sky, what do you see? Look into the field, the garden, the streets you roam about. Hear the childrens' laughter. Take a deep breath, as you do feel your lungs fill up with air. In this very moment as you exhale, feel the weight on your heart be released with your exhalation. Not for one moment did you ever wonder if your next breath of air was going to come or not. Joy is what you are therefore seeking.... but yet and still it's all around you. If you can't see it with your physical eyes, how are you going to perceive it with your spiritual senses? Start where you are planted first, then God will excel you to newer higher and heights. If you so as much can't start here, ask for a sense of direction in prayer. If you fail to do this joy will always elude you.

Jehovah is a happy God. To give you joy makes HIM joyous. He is also generous and kind and gives freely. If you ask for joy in abundance, then in the name of Jesus it's YES and Amen. The bible says you have not because you ask not. You have joy in great volumes. Myriads and myriads of joy is all around you in that place. The very secret hiding place of Jehovah. No one can penetrate your contentment or enter into your inner sanctum or sanctuary. For you yourself would have a circle formed around about you, for only you and your Creator. That you have personally formed by your bond with HIM. HIM in whom is shaping and molding the very person you are. Whom is refining you like fine gold and removing the dross off of your very being. This ONE yes the Grand Creator who created all things has entertained you day and night to the ambiance of sweet melody of joy with laughter as it's kinsmen and happiness as it's lodging place. Reclining together in the bosom position of his undeserved kindness. There was nothing we ever had to do to get here, but except Jesus invitation to come be his follower. We are certainly privileged to serve such an awesome God such as Jehovah.

Tragically people grow up in families and never receive a blessing or live with a marriage partner but never feel their approval or go through an entire school year and not feel accepted by teachers or, even worse, their peers.

Everyone wants and needs a blessing. An Old Testament story illustrates this quite well. Isaac had two sons, Esau and Jacob. Nearing the end of his life, Isaac wanted to give his blessing to his oldest son, Esau. But Jacob, through the conniving of his mother, tricked Isaac into giving him the blessing that was intended for Esau. When Esau heard that his father had blessed Jacob, "He cried out with a loud and bitter cry and said to his father, "'Bless me—me too, my father! . . . Isn't he rightly named Jacob? For he has cheated me twice now. He took my birthright, and look, now he has taken my blessing.' Then he asked, 'Haven't you saved a blessing for me?' . . . 'Do you only have one blessing, my father? Bless me—me too, my father! And Esau wept loudly'" (Gen. 27:34, 36, 38).

There is not enough emphasis in my words to properly communicate what was in Esau's voice when he said, "Bless me too, my father." This is the cry of every child to his or her parents. This is the cry of every spouse to his or her mate. This was the cry of boy and girl the cry of every woman or man. This is the cry of people you rub shoulders with every day. It may even be your cry.

Genuine acceptance is an unmet need in so many people today, but it does not have to be that way. You can give a blessing to those people. Heres how:

I. A blessing needs to be felt.

In the Scriptures, touch played an important part in the bestowal of the family blessing. When Isaac blessed Jacob, an embrace and a kiss were involved. The same is true today. We want and, often, need to feel the embrace of those we love.

It's an old story, but its truth transcends to time now. A little four-year-old girl became frightened late one night during a thunderstorm. After one particularly loud clap of thunder, she jumped up from her bed, ran down the hall, and burst into her parent's room. Jumping right in the middle of the bed, she sought out her parent's arms for comfort and reassurance. "Don't worry, honey," her father said, trying to calm her fears. "The Lord will protect you."

The little girl snuggled closer to her father and said, "I know that, Daddy, but right now I need someone with skin on!"

This little girl did not doubt her heavenly Father's ability to protect her, but she was also aware that he had given her an earthly father she could run to: someone whom God had entrusted with a special gift that could bring her comfort, security, and personal acceptance—the blessing of meaningful touch.

As a teenager, I desperately wanted to please my older brother. Kerry has a unique way of making people feel special. He is a bit different, but extremely a gentleman, the most kind-hearted person I've ever known. Through my adolescence he was the best friend I ever had, I vividly recall the times I would be in the house alone and he would come and take me with him to play outside. Instead of scolding me, he would place his enveloping hand on my shoulder, and explain my mistake, and then offer instruction for improvement. His touch communicated acceptance in spite of disappointment, no matter what it was. This meant a lot to me especially being the only girl. Not just that, but also being a public object of interest due to my partial left hand.

Have you ever noticed how often the Biblical writers speak of Jesus touching people? He touched the sick, the lepers, the blind, the deaf, the prostitutes, the outcasts. A tender moment in the life of Christ was when the children came to him. "Some people were bringing little children to him so he might touch them, but his disciples rebuked them. When Jesus saw it, He was indignant and said to them, "Let the little children come to me. Don't stop them, for the kingdom of God belongs to such as these. I assure you: Whoever does not welcome the kingdom of God like a little child will never enter it." After taking them in his arms, he laid His hands on them and healed them." (Mark 10:13-16). Jesus modeled for us the communication of a blessing through touch.

Never stop giving meaningful touches. Hugs, holding hands, the stroke of a head, and the arm around a shoulder all communicate acceptance, approval, importance and value. To neglect meaningful touch is to fail to transmit the blessing to others.

II. A blessing needs to be spoken

In the Scriptures the family blessing hinged, also, on a spoken message. Abraham spoke a blessing to Isaac. Isaac spoke it to his son Jacob. "When Isaac smelled his clothes, he blessed him. He came near, and kissed him. He smelled the smell of his clothing, and blessed him, and said, "Behold, the smell of my son is as the smell of a field which Yahweh has blessed.. . ." (Gen. 27:27). Jacob spoke it to each of his twelve sons and to two of his grandchildren. You see, a blessing is not a blessing unless it is spoken.

I have had constant affirmations. I needed those words then. I still need them now. Great power is manifested in words. "Life and death are in the power of the tongue, and those who love it will eat its fruit" (Prov. 18:21). Words have the incredible power to build us up or tear us down. The saying, "Sticks and stones may break my bones, but words will never hurt me," is an absolute lie. Words have the power of death. They inflict pain. They can destroy a friendship, rip apart a home, or cause harm in a marriage. And when these harmful words are spoken, it is almost impossible to take them back. They become like feathers in the wind.

Yet, on the other hand, words have the undeniable power to build people up. Words can be the source of healing, forgiveness, and life. Our children, our spouse, our friends, our work mates—everyone we rub shoulders with—long to hear words of approval, acceptance, and affection. And, let me add, they need to hear words of commendation before and after they have made a mistake or gotten into trouble. With the spoken blessing, we express the value and worth of the individual. Believe me, everyone you know longs to hear such phrases as, "I love you." "You are important to me." "You are going to make a difference in this world one day." "Knowing you makes my life complete!" These are words thar can change any one's day around, even their life.

Begin today, communicating your blessing to others. Especially your children, if you have them. One great tragedy in life is that we wait until it is too late to say how we feel about people we love. We will travel miles for a funeral to visit the dead before we go around the corner to visit someone alive and well. The Scriptures say, "When it is in your power, don't withhold good from the one to whom it is due. Don't say to your neighbor, "Go away! Come back later. I'll give it tomorrow'—when it is there with you today" (Prov. 3:27-28). Have you ever been to a family reunion? For most of the time people will talk about sports, recipes, movies, or the latest news events. But something happens the last hour of the reunion. Suddenly, before the family members say their good-byes, meaningful words will be spoken. A brother will say in private to his sister, "I know things will work out in your marriage. I'll be praying for you." An aunt will say to her niece, "You've always made me proud. I know school is hard, but you can do it. I believe in you." Or a daughter will say to a mother, "Look around you, Mom. We didn't turn out half bad, did we? We have you and Dad to thank." So often the most meaningful words are said just before the good-byes. Sometimes when we wait, we wait too long. And those words we wanted to say, or wanted to hear, are lost forever.

III. A blessing attaches special value to the person.

When we value something we place great importance on it. This is at the heart of the concept of blessing. In Hebrew, to "bow the knee" is the root meaning of blessing. This root word is used of a man who has his camel bend his knee so he could get on. In relationship to God the word came to mean "to adore with bended knees." Bowing before someone is a graphic picture of valuing that person. Anytime we bless someone, we are attaching high value to him or her.

Isaac placed great value on Jacob when he blessed him. He said, "So he came closer and kissed him. When Isaac smelled his clothes, he blessed him and said: 'Ah, the smell of my son is like the smell of a field that the LORD has blessed. May God give to you—from the dew of the sky and from the richness of the land—an abundance of grain and new wine. May peoples serve you and nations bow down to you. Be master over your brothers; may your mother's sons bow down to you. Those who curse you will be cursed, and those who bless you will be blessed" (Gen. 27:27-29). When Isaac told Jacob he smelled like a field he was communicating to his son that he was as refreshing as a newly cut field of hay or wheat. These were words of value to Jacob. First, Isaac was painting a picture for his son that one day other people would bow down to him. Second, it was a reminder that he would be a man of great respect because he was valuable. We can't miss the idea in these two pictures of praise that Jacob's father thought he was very valuable, someone who had great worth.

To express words of high value in some people we don't have to look very deep or very far. But for others it means that sometimes we must dig deep to discover the value of that individual. Sometimes it means that we must see what others do not see. We must see their potential and point it out to that individual. I love Michelangelo's response to the question, "How do you sculpture such beautiful angels?" He replied, "I see the angel in the marble and chisel until I set it free." That is what we must do with some people. We must look beyond the surface. We must point out a person's worth and value, and in doing so, we have the power to set them free. That's giving a blessing Henceforth, we try to hold on to a relationship for the sake of, wanting a certain outcome. However, in reality it may not come to pass. Bless the situation by releasing the person. You may stifle their growth, by clinging on. Allow a person to change on their on merits.

This is what Jesus did for Peter. Peter was called Simon before Jesus entered his life. Simon was a rough and tough fisherman who was unstable and insecure. Jesus came along and called him Peter, or Rock, and those words changed his life. Before, he was more like shifting sand. But one word of hope and Jesus pointed out his value, which henceforth created a man as strong and stable as a rock.

You can turn someone's life around by giving them a blessing. Through meaningful touch, a spoken word, and pointing out their value. Believe it or not you have the power to change the direction of someone's life, just by the words you choose to utter..

Conclusion

Perhaps you have come to adulthood and don't feel blessed. Your parents may never be able to bless you, but there is a heavenly Father anxious to bless you. You don't have to come, like Jacob and Esau deceiving God, pretending you are someone else. You can come just like you are, feeling inadequate or like a failure, knowing you are a sinner, and God will love you, forgive you, and accept you, and make you his child and bless you. The story of Jesus Christ is one way how God touches us and communicates his blessing to us.

"Do not grieve for the joy of the LORD is your strength."

Nehemiah 8:10b

The Subconscious can't Take a Joke

The subconscious can't take a joke.

The terrain beneath our conscious awareness is often referred to as the subconscious. Some have referenced this sub-terrain as the repository for the thousands or even millions of bits of information that are not normally processed by the conscious mind. This information is always there and can be called up to the surface using certain modalities. It also seems interesting that one mode of accessing the subconscious information database is through repetition of words. Some use affirmations and prayer.

Here's a thought provoking illustration as to how the subconscious became a faithful manifesting agent.

In Joseph Murphy's classic book, The Power of Your Subconscious Mind, originally published in 1963, he tells of the true story of a man whose daughter suffered from a debilitating form of arthritis and an incurable skin disease. With an intense desire to see his daughter healed from the pair of chronic and painful conditions, he would repeat the phrase "I would give my right arm to see my daughter cured." This he would reiterate consistently for a period of about two years.

One day while he and his family were out in their car, they collided with that of another car resulting in a terrible accident. The father's right arm was torn off at the shoulder. In a strange but miraculous twist, shortly thereafter his daughter's "incurable" conditions suddenly and permanently cleared up! Murphy says, "Remember that your subconscious mind cannot take a joke. It takes you at your word."

The bottom line on this rather tragic but miraculous story is that it seems that our subconscious can act as a faithful servant; bringing to fruition that which it is told, especially when the commands are repeated and delivered with passion! Metaphorically speaking – it has brought the fruits of its labor! Despite the fact that the father used a common phrase within the modern vernacular, he did not realize that the literal message he was feeding to his subconscious would result in an actual reality he would experience – this is the power of suggestion!

There's an ole adage that states "Say what you mean and mean what you say." These are words spoken true. So unless you want to see the evidence of the reality, don't speak just mere words just to be saying them. Remember, the subconscious mind cannot distinguish between a truth or a joke. It always takes you at your word. Speak words of positivity as often as possible. There's another saying "Hope for the best, but prepare for the worst!" Now correct me if I'm wrong for being so blunt, but you're always going to get exactly what you are preparing for. Everything has a vibration in which things are attracted to it. In other words, it sort of becomes a self fulfilling prophesy. You cannot expect the best if you already have convinced yourself that the worst is what is bound to happen. That's like putting cyanide in filtered water and hoping that somehow you drink only the portion the cyanide hasn't poisoned! Ridiculous thinking right?

So change the phrase to "no matter what happens, only the best can come from it!" In turn you are telling the Universe, God and HIS angels that no matter what comes your way, rather it's for good or for bad, that YOU will only draw for the positive. In doing this you are attracting your good to you, in unpanelled form. You are not forcing God"s hand by expecting nothing but the best for yourself in your life. Trust me HE is more than up for the challenge. You can never exhaust HIS resources. HE has an Infinite Supply that you can never deplete, no matter how much you acquire from it. So GO ahead and tap into this resource by having faith that come what may, only the best is in store for you and your life. We have been so conditioned to think negative all the time, that we think that it's normal. When really we are a far cry from help. However, we need to retrain our minds to serve us for our greater good, than for our demise. Never should we underestimate the power of a strong focused well directed mind.

"Every day in every way, I am getting better and better."

-Emile Coue

Saying these words everyday will eventually become your sudden reality. Become the master of your own thoughts. Do not leave it to chance or to others to do your thinking for you. Be in control over your own life. For what it's worth in the end, you're the only one that has to live with the consequences of your actions.

Fertilize the Sub-terrain With Conscious Thought

Fertilize the sub-terrain with conscious thoughts

If this is the matrix for which reality creation on the physical plane works, imagine what one can do by directing conscious messages to the subterranean levels of the mind? The conscious mind is the Watchman. He stands at the gate to guard the subconscious mind from harmful thoughts. If we don't train this soldier well then our garrison will be compromised and quickly overthrown, from outside intrusions. These intruders will rob you of your peace of mind and ruin good relationships. They also will impress upon your mind things that will hold you hostage in your own movie called "life!" You will literally be a POYOM, a Prisoner Of Your Own Mind! With that being said take charge by thinking. Yes, I know it sounds so simple, but do you know that most people do not think? They let their minds run in autopilot for as long as they get by in life, they don't start weighing their thoughts carefully until it's often too late!

Being the habitual creatures that we are phrases we use and the behaviors we exhibit are often the result of learned responses. Further, we live in a world where messages of "lack and limitation" unfortunately are predominate in our daily lives. It can therefore be difficult to train the mind chatter to turn from "I can't" to "I can." However there are techniques in which we can plant fertile seeds in the mind in order to germinate our desires more effectively.

A good way of dong this is through the use of affirmations. "I know that this may not be what I expected, however, I know that what I really want is coming." This is a good affirmation to repeat before bed when you have met with a barrage of problems. Many of us face complexities. None of us are exempt. It's all about how we approach the situation, that results in the outcome. If you continue to plant in the fertile soil of your mind, positive thoughts, then you can even expect in a not to great circumstance, a more favorable conclusion.

If you fall sick, instead of saying "what next?" try saying "It is well with me, I see myself getting better each day."' You have the power to create and shape your life. God is not punishing you for what you so called did in a past life and asking for retribution. We do reap what we sow, in this life time. The wages that sin pays is death. After death comes your acquittal of your sins. Your debt is paid in full by means of Jesus Christ's ransom.

Thinking is the first step into forming our reality. Whether we're wrong or right or form our own opinions and become indifferent, a person, has every opportunity, to settle the score now. We need to cleanse our mind by placing new thoughts in it. We will learn more on how to do exactly that in the next chapter.

Planting New Thought Seeds

Planting New Thought seeds

Prior to going to sleep, think of a phrase or affirmation that represents something you would like to see manifest. "All of my relationships are healthy and whole." Or "I am so happy that I am now financially independent." Whatever the phrase, make it genuine - one hundred percent organic. And make it short and sweet! Say it out loud and then gradually as you begin to get drowsy, take it down to a whisper, until this is the only phrase occupying your mind. Put it in your heart and feel the power of your heart receiving as if it were happening as you speak it. The temptation to retreat back to that other voice that's saying "you can't" or "you know this is not't true," may feel intractable but be insistent on feeling the reality of the phrase you are saying. Pull the weeds of self-doubt out of the soil and replace them with good seeds! Your conscious mind is receiving the data and once you fall asleep, that data will then sink into the subconscious– doing its best to see to it that proper seeds sprout. It pays to be persistent in this pursuit. Remember, we are training our minds to think in a different way and thus dig up the weeds that have become far too overgrown!

Now that we're approaching spring time in our minds - a time when we prepare to plant new seeds in hopes of a fruitful harvest, let us not forget the what we plant in the mind will spring forth in perfect accord, just like the buds we'll soon see peaking through the soil in the Spring season. The good news is we are the gardeners and we have the ability to create a reality brimming with the fruits we have so desired as long as we're mindful that what we are planting is what we truly wish to see.

"In order to get something you never had, you have to do something you've never done"

Nothing is more exciting than seeing your seed turn into something that blooms.

Here are a few things to keep in mind as you start planting seeds in your own life:

1. Seeds take time to grow.

A whole garden is not created over night, and neither is a dream life.

But, by focusing on the positives, and seeing the little seeds that start to peek out from the earth in the form of something new, we can start to see the progress we are making in our journey to start living the life we're have always wanted.

2. Seeds must change in order to grow.

A seed can't stay a seed forever. When cared for with nourishing soil, rays of sunlight, and water, they change shape and start to become whatever it is they were meant to be.

To really experience positive change, you too, must let go of your past and embrace the transformation that's about to take place. Have confidence knowing you will take on a better form, even if it takes time.

3. When a seed flowers, everyone recognizes its beauty.

After a seed undergoes a transformation and takes on a new form, everyone appreciates it for whatever it has to offer, whether it's a smile-inducing lotus flower or a crisp apple.

Each seed has something new, something more to contribute. And how did it get to this point? With time and a transformative change.

Go out there and start planting seeds in your life, no matter how hard or pointless it may seem right now. With a little time, patience and hard work, what now seems like an empty dirt plot will be filled with beauty and growth.

Just like a beautiful flower attracts butterflies, your life will be a magnet to the right kind of people that will truly make it one worth living.

"Don't judge each day by the harvest you reap but by the seeds that you plant."

— Robert Louis Stevenson

During my life I have heard people ridicule others for being rich or wealthy, that were poor. Saying things like a "camel has a better chance getting through a needle of an eye, before a rich man gets into heaven." Rightly so it is in the bible, however it doesn't give you the right to use it to bring condemnation upon another. In fact lets delve into why this scripture carries a much larger impact. In Jesus illustration here he used it because most rich people are more concerned about their riches and their protection of it than dedicating time and effort in serving God, or pursuing HIS kingdom. Does this mean that all rich people are like this? No. In fact there are some poor people who still slave for riches and will not make it neither. There also exist among the rich those who truly love Jehovah and have dedicated a life of service to his kingdom. So never think that by choosing to stay famished financially, God some how will have some type of obligation of mercy on you and overlook your errors. Contrary to belief there's no virtue in poverty my dear. In fact it is not of God to be in lack of anything at all. The 23rd Psalms gives us evidence of this. To avoid this never judge. Galatians 6:7&8 Do not be misled: God is not one to be mocked. For what ever a person is sowing, this he will also reap; because the one sowing with a view to his flesh will reap corruption from his flesh, but the one showing with a view to the spirit will reap everlasting life from the spirit. I'm saying this to say, don't believe the hype. I know some pretty affluent people in my life, from all backgrounds and religion. They all got something in common, they all are givers. Those who give without feeling resentful but cheerful reap a bountiful harvest. The more you give with the right intention the more that things have a way of showing up, unexpected. Rest assure that Jesus was rich spiritually. It's worthy to note that one is rich spiritually before it's ever manifested physically. As far as I'm concerned Jesus was the richest man that ever walked the face of the earth. For one no one could buy what he had because it was not't for sale and he was the only person who had it! If we all had what we he had, we would never worry where we were going to get our next bread and butter from period!

Names of people in the bible that were rich:

1. Probably the first rich person mentioned in the Scriptures is **Abram**. Genesis 13:2 says "Abram was very rich in livestock, silver and gold."

2. Also in Genesis is a reference to another rich person in Scripture. Read Genesis 26:12-15 and see that **Isaac**, like his father, "became a rich man and his wealth only continued to grow. He acquired large flocks of sheep and goats, great herds of cattle and many servants." Read the rest. The Philistines were so jealous that they filled his wells with dirt and told him to move. What was the reason they wanted him to move? He had become too rich and too powerful for them.

3. **Nah-ab** was also very wealthy as we see from I Samuel 25. Although David's men had been protecting **Nahab's** shepherds, and it was the custom in those days for travelers to be given provisions, **Nah-ab**, with all his riches, refused to give provisions to David and his men. Guess that is why he got the reputation of being the stingy, wealthy man.

4. Now **Solomon** became richer and wiser than any other king on earth according to I Kings 10:23. He was also the King who asked God for wisdom. The Scriptures say that "year after year every nation came to consult him and to hear the wisdom God had given him. Year after year everyone who visited brought him gifts of silver and gold, clothing, weapons, spices, horses and mules."

5. **Jehoshaphat** was a king in Judah. He was a good king who did not worship the images of Baal and obeyed the commands of the

Lord. The Lord blessed him and all the people loved and respected him so much that they brought him gifts. They gave him so much, in fact, that he became very rich. This is chronicled in II Chronicles 17:3-5.

6. Look at II Chronicles 32:27-29. That Scripture is about **Hezekiah**, who was so rich he had to build special treasury buildings for all his silver, gold, precious stones and spices, his shields and other valuable items. He even built more buildings to hold all his grain, wine, olive oil, cattle, sheep and goats. Now that is rich!

7. If you are familiar with the Book of Esther, you may remember **King Xerxes.** He is also known by **Ahasuerus.** He threw a banquet that lasted 180 days. Yes, it lasted six months. Obviously he had some riches of which he could dispose. You find his story in Esther 1.

8. **Job** is a man who is rich when we first meet him in Job 1. He quickly loses it all but not because of anything he did. By Chapter 42, we see the Lord restores Job's fortune and gives him twice as much as before. Read the whole book to get the full story on Job and his wealth.

9. Last, we look at a New Testament man by the name of **Zacchaeus.** He was a tax collector by trade and not very popular with the people. It was well known that the tax collectors gouged the people but all those taxes put **Zacchaeus** on our list of the top nine rich people in Scripture. The **Zacchaeus** account is in Luke 19 so you can read it yourself.

There is an account in Matthew where Jesus speaks with a "rich," **young ruler**. Jesus tells him to go and sell all his possessions and give the money to the poor and that he would have treasures in heaven. He goes away troubled. Jesus then says "I tell you the truth, it is very hard for a rich person to enter the Kingdom of Heaven."

Read the full accounts of the rich people listed above. Some of them had trouble because of the wealth they acquired. Some did not. The Bible does not say that money is the root of all evil but the LOVE of money is. These Scriptures make for some interesting reading about how each rich man reacted to his wealth. Which goes to show that there is completely no virtue in poverty, nor should one be condemned for having wealth.

Sowing Seeds of Thought

Sowing Seeds of Thought

One of the most important principals for achieving success is to understand that your mind is like a garden bed where you cultivate and grow the seeds of thought.

When you plant a positive seed of thought in your mind and nurture it carefully, it germinates and grows until it leads you to take action.

As soon as you begin acting on your idea, your seed of positive thought becomes a seedling of positive action.

If you continue to feed and encourage this seedling, it gradually develops into a tree of positive habit. With branches of productivity, equipped for the work at hand.

Once this habit has become solid and immovable, it is then only a matter of time before it blossoms to produce the fruits of success.

However it is important to be aware that the garden of your mind does not discriminate between positive and negative seeds of thought.

A negative seed of thought planted within your mind often leads you to take negative actions. These actions gradually develop into negative habits that will inevitably produce the fruits of failure.

When you understand that your thoughts lead to actions and your actions develop into habits and that it is your habits that determine your results in life, then you'll appreciate why it's so important to be careful about the seeds of thought that you plant within your mind.

One of the real secrets of success is to become a watchful caretaker over the garden of your mind and make sure that you only plant and cultivate thoughts that will develop into the positive habits necessary for making your dreams a reality.

So what does this mean in the real world?

It means that you should carefully monitor the thoughts that you are planting within your mind each day. You should regularly be taking inventory. Whenever you catch yourself planting or nurturing a negative thought, make the conscious decision to uproot and discard it.

For example, when Alex went to see his doctor, he was told that he had high cholesterol and needed to lose 20lbs. In response to this advice, Alex joined his local gym and started exercising three days a week.

A few weeks later Alex stood in front of his bed room mirror and assessed his reflection.

His first thought was, "I look exactly the same! All that hard work and I don't look any different. This is not't working at all."

Then he stopped and realized that this was a negative seed of thought.

He knew that if he continued to nurture this negative perspective it would not't be long before he started skipping sessions and pretty soon his exercise program would be a thing of the past.

Having recognized his negative seed of thought, Alex made the conscious decision to uproot and discard it before it took hold in his mind.

He took a second look at his reflection and told himself, "Every training session is making me fitter." This was a positive seed of thought that made him feel good about the action he was taking.

Over time, he continued his training program while protecting his mind from the disempowering seeds of negativity. Eventually Alex reached his goal weight and brought his cholesterol level down to a healthy level.

So today I'd like to encourage you to become a watchful caretaker of your mind. Whenever you identify a seed of negative thought, uproot and discard it.

Remember, it is much easier to uproot a seed of negative thought than it is to chop down a tree of negative habit that has taken root over many years.

By planting and cultivating seeds of positive thought, you will set in motion a truly remarkable process.

In the same way that a tiny acorn develops into a mighty oak tree, your positive seeds of thought will germinate into the actions and habits that will ultimately lead you to success.

Here in a few cryptic words is a concise and specific direction for making use of the creative power of thought by impressing upon the subconscious the particular thing you desire. Your thought, idea, plan, or purpose is as real on its own plane as your hand or your heart. In following the biblical technique, you completely eliminate from your mind all consideration of conditions, circumstances, or anything that might imply a negative outcome. You are planting a seed (concept) in the mind that, if you leave it undisturbed, will infallibly germinate into external fruition. The prime condition that Jesus insisted upon was faith. Over and over again you read in the Bible, According to your faith is it done unto you. If you plant certain types of seeds in the ground, you have faith they will grow after their kind. This is the way of seeds, and trusting the laws of growth and agriculture, you know that the seeds will come forth after their kind. The faith that is described in the Bible is a way of thinking, an attitude of mind, an inner certitude, knowing that the idea you fully accept in your conscious mind will be embodied in your subconscious mind and made manifest. Faith is, in a sense, accepting as true what your reason and senses deny. It is dosing down, refusing to listen to the little, rational, analytic, conscious mind and embracing an attitude of complete reliance on the inner power of your subconscious mind.

Here is one of the best known examples of the biblical technique of healing: And when he came into the house, the blind men came to him: and Jesus saith unto them, Believe ye that I am able to do this? They said unto him, Yea, Lord. Then touched he their eyes, saying, according to your faith be it unto you. And their eyes were opened; and Jesus straitly charged them, saying, see that no man know it.
MATT 9:28-30

By saying, according to your faith be it unto you, Jesus was openly appealing to the cooperation of the subconscious mind of the blind men. Their faith was their great expectancy, their inner feeling, their inner conviction that something miraculous would happen, that their prayer would be answered. And therefore it was. This is the time honored technique of healing, utilized alike by all healing groups throughout the world, regardless of religious affiliation. In saying, see that no man know it, Jesus was urging the healed patients not to discuss their healing with others. If they did so, they might be harassed by the skeptical and derogatory criticisms of the unbelieving. This in turn might have tended to undo the benefits they had received at the hand of Jesus by depositing thoughts of fear, doubt, and anxiety in the subconscious mind.

"Fruits doesn't fall far from the tree but there seeds can go places and wherever they go by their virtues they leave their traces"

— Indira Mukhopadhyay

Sowing Seeds of Life

Sowing Seeds of Life

"Inside that tiny seed, lives the roots, branches, bark, trunk, leaves, twigs and apple fruit of that apple tree. You can't see, feel, hear, taste or smell any of that yet; nevertheless, it is all inside that seed. The moment the seed is in your hand— all of that is in your hand, too, from the root to the bark to the fruit! All you have to do is to push the seed into the soil. And what makes anyone plant any apple seed? It is the belief that in the seed, there is the tree. So, believe. To have a seed, is to have everything."

Here is a wonderful example of King David and King Saul.

"It is unthinkable, on my part, from Jehovah's standpoint, that I should do this thing to my lord, the anointed of Jehovah."
—1 Sam. 24:6.

After David fled from him, Saul took 3,000 chosen men out of all Israel and went looking for David in the wilderness. (1 Sam. 24:2) Eventually, Saul unknowingly went into the very cave where David and his men were. David could have used this opportunity to eliminate the king who threatened his life. After all, it was God's will for David to replace Saul as king of Israel. (1 Sam. 16: 1, 13) Indeed, if David had listened to the advice of his men, the king would have been killed. (1 Sam. 24:4-7) But Saul was still God's anointed king. David did not want; to rob Saul of the kingship, since Jehovah had not yet removed him. By only cutting off the skirt of Saul's sleeveless coat, David showed that he had no intention of harming Saul.—1 Sam. 24:11

Let us too have good intentions from the heart just like David had for Saul. In fact this was not the only time Saul intended to kill David. So David could have reasoned in his own heart, to avenge Saul before one of his attempts succeeds in David's demise. On the contrary David beckoned to Jehovah's call. He knew that Jehovah's words would prove faithful and true of him being the next successor on the throne. By killing Saul David could have sped up his time for reigning as the new king of Israel.

Instead he sowed a seed of life by sparing Saul's. You may be going through something just as taxing as David. Someone may not be seeking to kill your literal soul, however they may perhaps be out to destroy your person or your character and even your reputation. The bible says "Return evil for evil to no one." Vengeance belongs to God, not man. Just like David did Saul spare them. Don't go around justifying what they said, don't even try to defend your own honor. Why not, you may exclaim? The reason is this, the truth doesn't need to be defended, it just needs to be upheld. In the meantime keep your composure. Maintain your personal integrity and in the grand scheme of things Jehovah will exult you in due time. It may be in a even higher position than the one you held previously. It is good to continue breathing life in others. Sowing the seeds of life promotes a better quality of life for us now and the years to come.

The Story of Abigail

The story of Abigail

One such woman was Abigail, wife of the wealthy Israelite landowner Nabal. Abigail's sensibleness contributed to the saving of lives and prevented David, Israel's future king, from becoming bloodguilty.

This is how it all begun:

ABIGAIL saw the panic in the young man's eyes. He was terrified—and for good reason. Grave danger loomed. Right at that moment, some 400 warriors were on the way, determined to kill off every male in the household of Nabal, Abigail's husband. Why?

It had all started with Nabal. He had acted cruelly and insolently, as usual. This time, though, he had insulted the wrong man—the beloved commander of a loyal and well-trained band of warriors. Now, one of Nabal's young workmen, perhaps a shepherd, came to Abigail, trusting that she would come up with a plan to save them. But what could one woman do against an army?

First, let us learn a little more about this remarkable woman. Who was Abigail? How had this crisis arisen? And what can we learn from her example of faith?

Abigail and Nabal were not a good match. Nabal could hardly have chosen a better spouse, whereas Abigail found herself married to one who could hardly have been worse. Granted, the man had money. He thus saw himself as very important, but how did others view him? It would be difficult to find a Bible character who is spoken of in more contemptuous terms. His very name means "Senseless," or "Stupid." Did his parents give him such a name at birth, or was it an epithet that stuck to him later? In either case, he lived up to his name. Nabal was "harsh and bad in his practices." A bully and a drunkard, he was widely feared and disliked.—1 Sam. 25:2, 3, 17, 21, 25.

Abigail was altogether different from Nabal. Her name means "My Father Has Made Himself Joyful." Many a father is proud to have a beautiful daughter, but a wise father is far happier to discern inner beauty in his child. All too often, a person blessed with outward beauty fails to see the need to develop such qualities as discretion, wisdom, courage, or faith. Not so with Abigail. The Bible praises her for her discretion as well as for her beauty.- -Read 1 25:3

Some today might wonder why such an intelligent young woman married such a good-for-nothing man. Remember, many marriages in Bible times were arranged. If not, parental consent was still of great importance. Did Abigail's parents favor this marriage, even arrange it, because they were impressed with Nabal's wealth and prominence? Did they feel pressured by poverty? At any rate, Nabal's money did not make him a fit husband.

Wise parents carefully teach their children a wholesome view of marriage. They neither urge their children to marry for money nor pressure them to begin dating when still too young to take on adult roles and responsibilities. (1 Cor. 7:36) However, it was too late for Abigail to think about such things. For whatever reason, she was married to Nabal, and she was determined to make the best of a difficult situation.

Nabal had just made Abigail's situation harder than ever. The man he had insulted was none other than David. This was the faithful servant of Jehovah whom Samuel the prophet had anointed, revealing David as God's choice to succeed Saul as king. (1 Sam. 16:1, 2, 11-13) On the run from the jealous and murderous King Saul, David was dwelling in the wilderness with his 600 loyal warriors.

Nabal lived in Maon but worked and likely owned land in nearby Carmel.* Those towns lay a midst grassy uplands suitable for raising sheep, of which Nabal owned 3,000. All around, though, was wild country. To the south lay the vast wilderness of Paran. To the east, the approach to the Salt Sea led through desolate wastelands riddled with ravines and caves. In these regions David and his men struggled to survive, no doubt hunting for their food and enduring many hardships. They often encountered the young men who worked as shepherds for the wealthy Nabal.

How did those hardworking soldiers treat the shepherds? It would have been easy for them to help themselves to a sheep now and then, but they did nothing of the kind. On the contrary, they were like a protective wall around Nabal's flocks and servants. Read 1 Samuel 25:15, Sheep and shepherds faced plenty of dangers. Predators abounded, and Israel's southern border was so close that bands of foreign marauders and thieves frequently attacked.*

It must have been quite an undertaking to keep all those men fed in the wilderness. So one day David sent ten messengers to Nabal to ask for help. David chose the moment wisely. It was the festive time of sheepshearing, when generosity and feasting were customary. David also chose his words with care, using polite terms and forms of address. He even referred to himself as "your son David," perhaps a respectful acknowledgment of Nabal's greater age. How did Nabal respond?—1 Sam. 25:5-8.

He was outraged! "He screamed rebukes at them" is how the young man mentioned at the outset described the scene to Abigail. Miserly Nabal complained loudly about his precious bread, water, and slaughtered meat. He ridiculed David as inconsequential and compared him to a runaway servant. Nabal's view may have been similar to that of Saul, who hated David. Neither man had Jehovah's view. God loved David and saw him, not as a rebellious slave, but as the future king of Israel.—1 Sam. 25:10, 11, 14.

When the emissaries reported back to David, he became furious. "Gird on every one his sword!" he commanded. Arming himself, David led 400 of his men to attack. He vowed to wipe out every male in Nabal's household. (1 Sam. 25:12, 13, 21, 22) David's ire was understandable, but his way of expressing it was wrong. The Bible says: "Man's wrath does not work out God's righteousness." (Jas. 1:20) How, though, could Abigail save her household?

In a way, we have already seen Abigail take the first step toward righting this terrible wrong. Unlike her husband, Nabal, she proved willing to listen. As for bringing the matter to Nabal, the young servant said of him: "He is too much of a good-for-nothing fellow to speak to him."*(1 Sam. 25:17) Tragically, Nabal's view of his own importance rendered him unwilling to listen. Such arrogance is all too common even to this day. But the young man knew Abigail to be different, which is no doubt why he approached her with this problem.

Abigail thought and acted quickly. "At once Abigail hastened," we read. Four times in this one account we find the same verb, "to hasten," used regarding this woman. She prepared a generous gift for David and his men. It included bread, wine, sheep, roasted grain, cakes of raisins, and cakes of figs. Clearly, Abigail knew well what she had and was thoroughly in charge of her household responsibilities, much like the capable wife later described in the book of Proverbs. (Prov. 31:10-31) She sent the provisions ahead with some of her servants, then followed alone. "But," we read, "to her husband Nabal she told nothing."—1 Sam. 25:18, 19.

Does this mean that Abigail was rebelling against her husband's rightful headship? No; keep in mind that Nabal had acted wickedly against an anointed servant of Jehovah, an action that could well result in death for many innocent members of Nabal's household. If Abigail failed to act, might she become a sharer in her husband's guilt? In this case, she had to put submission to her God ahead of submission to her husband.

Before long, Abigail met up with David and his men. Again she hastened, this time to descend from her donkey and humble herself before David. (1 Sam. 25:20, 23) Then she poured out her heart at length, making a powerful plea for mercy in behalf of her husband and her household. What made her words effective?

She took responsibility for the problem and asked David to forgive her personally. She realistically acknowledged that her husband was as senseless as his name implied, perhaps suggesting that it would be beneath David's dignity to chastise such a man. She expressed her trust in David as Jehovah's representative, recognizing that he was fighting "the wars of Jehovah." She also indicated that she knew of Jehovah's promise regarding David and the kingship, for she said: "Jehovah . . . certainly will commission you as leader over Israel." Further, she urged David not to take any action that might bring bloodguilt upon him or that might later become "a cause for staggering"—evidently referring to a troubled conscience. Read 1 25:24-31 Kind, moving words!

And how did David respond? He accepted what Abigail had brought and said: "Blessed be Jehovah the God of Israel, who has sent you this day to meet me! And blessed be your sensibleness, and blessed be you who have restrained me this day from entering into bloodguilt." David praised her for bravely hastening to meet him, and he acknowledged that she had restrained him from incurring bloodguilt. "Go up in peace to your house," he told her, and he humbly added: "I have listened to your voice."—1 Sam. 25:32-35.

After she took her leave, Abigail could not help thinking about that meeting; nor could she have failed to notice the contrast between that faithful, kind man and the brute to whom she was married. But she did not dwell on such thoughts. We read: "Later Abigail came in to Nabal." Yes, she returned to her husband as determined as ever to carry out her role as his wife to the best of her ability. She had to tell him of the gift she had given to David and his men. He had a right to know. She also had to tell him—before he learned of it elsewhere, to his even greater shame—about the danger that had been averted. She could not tell him now though. He was feasting like a king and was as drunk as could be.—1 Sam. 25:36.

Again showing both courage and discretion, she waited until the next morning when the influence of the wine had ebbed. He would be sober enough to understand her, yet possibly more dangerous in his temper as well. Still, she approached and told him the whole story. No doubt she expected him to explode in fury, perhaps violence. Instead, he just sat there, not moving.—1 Sam. 25:37.

What was wrong with the man? "His heart came to be dead inside him, and he himself became as a stone." Perhaps he had suffered some form of stroke. However, about ten days later, his end came—and not strictly for medical reasons. The account tells us: "Jehovah struck Nabal, so that he died." (1 Sam. 25:38) With that righteous execution, Abigail's long nightmare of a marriage was over. While Jehovah does not step in with miraculous executions today, this account is a fitting reminder that no case of domestic tyranny or abuse escapes his notice. In his own time, he will always bring about justice.—Read Luke 8:17

Besides the release from a bad marriage, Abigail had another blessing in store. When he learned of the death of Nabal, David sent messengers to propose marriage. "Here is your slave girl," she responded, "as a maidservant to wash the feet of the servants of my lord." Clearly, she was not changed by the prospect of becoming David's wife; she even offered to be a servant to his servants! Then we read again of her hastening, this time to ready herself to go to David.—1 Sam. 25:39-42.

This was no fairy-tale ending; Abigail's life with David would not always be easy. David was already married to Ahinoam, and though God permitted polygamy, it surely presented special challenges to faithful women back then. And David was not yet king; there would be obstacles and hardships to surmount before he served Jehovah in that way. But as Abigail helped and supported David along life's road, eventually bearing him a son, she learned that she had a husband who valued her and protected her. On one occasion he even rescued her from kidnappers! (1 Sam. 30:1-19) David thus imitated Jehovah God, who loves and values such discreet, courageous, and faithful women.

The account of Abigail is noteworthy of our undivided attention. If we peers deeply beneath the surface from the letters penned down about her we will begin to see the value of cultivation in the right soil. Abigail saved her husband's life, however as we learned through his own inactions he met with death any how. Abigail did her part. In this ordeal she didn't know she was setting her self up for something greater than what she had originally anticipated.

She in fact gave her husband a second chance to uproot his bad seeds and put in it's place good seeds. In contrast her husband was not brought to his senses through his wife's own heroic act of risking her own life to save him.

Instead he kept sowing bad seeds in which yielded him bad fruits.

For instance let's take modern day society. We all know that no matter where you live on the globe it is forbade to drink and drive. Therefore you would think that as law abiding citizens we would submit to this law. There may be someone who shirks at this law because they have been drinking and driving for years and had never even came close to a fender bender, let alone a right out full pledge accident. So this person may be thinking I have been writing with the same pen in life and it has served me until now, why would I change what doesn't need to be fixed? On the other hand you got another individual who never drinks and drive.

Now person A who has skillfully found a way to dodge the bullet on car accidents sets out to drive. As usual they are mentally impaired due to the alcohol levels. The second person B who never drinks and drive, starts off very slow and cautious because the roads are very icy and slippery. Coincidentally they both meet up. Person A is at a stoplight person B is breaking right behind person A, but ends up crashing in the back of person A's vehicle. Person B is bleeding, loosing large quantities of blood by the minute. Person A is fine but is slow in action to check on person B. Eventually person A realizes person B isn't moving, so immediately person A moves swiftly to inquire of the other driver. Upon approaching the vehicle of person B, person A discovers person B expired. The first thing person A thought was if I hadn't been drinking, I could have saved this person's life. Rather person A caused the accident or not person A is now a suspect in a crime scene. The police arrives at the scene, person A is clearly inebriated, how is person A going to dodge this bullet? So just like Nabal a person's actions will catch up with them rather they see the harm or not. God universal laws are not partisans. What goes for one person goes for all. Sometimes our actions or inactions; or our failure to act, can count against us.

If we know something is wrong and we continue to take part in it, then this makes us willing participants rather we realize it or not. So whatever penalty is earned, if we do not adhere to changing, it will encircle us as a noose tied around the neck of a criminal. This is certainly not a seed that I personally would like to sow. What a wonderful conclusion Abigail had. We too can come off victoriously, just as she did if we sow seeds of life even if it entails giving up a bad habit.

Sowing Seeds of Change

Sowing Seeds of Change

"Acceptance makes an incredible fertile soil for the seeds of change."

There Is a Time For Everything Including Change

"For everything there is an appointed time, even a time for every affair under the heavens," says the Bible. The writer of those words, the ancient wise King Solomon, went on to say that there is a time to be born and a time to die, a time to build and a time to tear down, a time to love and a time to hate. Finally, he observed: "What advantage is there for the doer in what he is working hard at?"—Ecclesiastes 3:1-9.

REMEMBER You cannot scale a mountain in a single step; however, you can take on the challenge one step at a time. The same is true of most obstacles you face, no matter how mountain-like they might seem to be.

THEIR CIRCUMSTANCES CHANGED

Consider four faithful people mentioned in the Bible who suffered despair to the point of not wanting to go on.

REBEKAH "If this is the way it is, why should I go on living?"—Genesis 25:22.

MOSES "Please kill me right now. . . . Do not make me see any more calamity."—Numbers 11:15.

ELIJAH "Take my life away, for I am no better than my forefathers."—1 Kings 19:4.

JOB "Why did I not die at birth?"—Job 3:11.

If you read the Bible accounts about these people, you will find that their circumstances changed for the better—and in ways that they could not have foreseen. The same might be true for you. (Ecclesiastes 11:6) Do not give up!

Guard Against
Seeds of Destruction

Guard Against Seeds of Destruction

Man has dominated man to his own injury

Ecclesiastes 8:9

Sometime in the mid-1970's, Henry Kissinger, a life-long practitioner of "Balance of Power" geopolitics and a man with more than a fair share of conspiracies under his belt, allegedly declared his blueprint for world domination: "Control the oil and you control nations. Control the food, and you control the people." Since the beginning of man, man has polluted his own mind into believing that domination and power over others is the ultimate goal of existence. The Bible clearly says that man would dominate man to his own injury. Now we the manifestation of these words spoken so true through Genetically Modified Organisms. pesticides, vaccinations, air & water pollution. Artificial Intelligence that control weather climates etc. This is just the short and skinny into what is going on in the world around us. If I had the time I could dedicate myself to writing a whole separate book on this discussion alone. My main focus is helping my readers in avoidance of these seeds of destruction. These concerns, however, need not fill us with gloom. Really, they just serve to illustrate a larger point. The Bible helps us to see that we should not expect too much from the imperfect humans currently managing this planet and its resources. For now, failures and mismanagement are simply part of the human condition. Hence, Psalm 146:3 advises: "Do not put your trust in nobles, nor in the son of earthling man, to whom no salvation belongs." But we can put our complete trust in God. (Proverbs 3:5, 6) He has both the desire and the power to help us.—Isaiah 40:25, 26.

News Media

News Media:

In the past few decades, the fortunate among us have recognised the hazards of living with an overabundance of food (obesity, diabetes) and have started to change our diets. But most of us do not yet understand that news is to the mind what sugar is to the body. News is easy to digest. The media feeds us small bites of trivial matter, tidbits that don't really concern our lives and don't require thinking. That's why we experience almost no saturation. Unlike reading books and long magazine articles (which require thinking), we can swallow limitless quantities of news flashes, which are bright-colored candies for the mind. Today, we have reached the same point in relation to information that we faced 20 years ago in regard to food. We are beginning to recognise how toxic news can be.

News misleads. Take the following event (borrowed from Nassim Taleb). A car drives over a bridge, and the bridge collapses. What does the news media focus on? The car. The person in the car. Where he came from. Where he planned to go. How he experienced the crash (if he survived). But that is all irrelevant. What's relevant? The structural stability of the bridge. That's the underlying risk that has been lurking, and could lurk in other bridges. But the car is flashy, it's dramatic, it's a person (non-abstract), and it's news that's cheap to produce. News leads us to walk around with the completely wrong risk map in our heads. So terrorism is over-rated. Chronic stress is under-rated. The collapse of Lehman Brothers is overrated. Fiscal irresponsibility is under-rated. Astronauts are over-rated. Nurses are under-rated.

We are not rational enough to be exposed to the press. Watching an airplane crash on television is going to change your attitude toward that risk, regardless of its real probability. If you think you can compensate with the strength of your own inner contemplation, you are wrong. Bankers and economists – who have powerful incentives to compensate for news-borne hazards – have shown that they cannot. The only solution: cut yourself off from news consumption entirely.

News is irrelevant. Out of the approximately 10,000 news stories you have read in the last 12 months, name one that – because you consumed it – allowed you to make a better decision about a serious matter affecting your life, your career or your business. The point is: the consumption of news is irrelevant to you. But people find it very difficult to recognise what's relevant. It's much easier to recognise what's new. The relevant versus the new is the fundamental battle of the current age. Media organization want you to believe that news offers you some sort of a competitive advantage. Many fall for that. We get anxious when we're cut off from the flow of news. In reality, news consumption is a competitive disadvantage. The less news you consume, the bigger the advantage you have.

News has no explanatory power. News items are bubbles popping on the surface of a deeper world. Will accumulating facts help you understand the world? Sadly, no. The relationship is inverted. The important stories are non-stories: slow, powerful movements that develop below journalists' radar but have a transforming effect. The more "news factoids" you digest, the less of the big picture you will understand. If more information leads to higher economic success, we'd expect journalists to be at the top of the pyramid. That's not the case.

News is toxic to your body. It constantly triggers the limbic system. Panicky stories spur the release of cascades of glucocorticoid (cortisol). This deregulates your immune system and inhibits the release of growth hormones. In other words, your body finds itself in a state of chronic stress. High glucocorticoid levels cause impaired digestion, lack of growth (cell, hair, bone), nervousness and susceptibility to infections. The other potential side-effects include fear, aggression, tunnel-vision and desensitization.

News increases cognitive errors. News feeds the mother of all cognitive errors: confirmation bias. In the words of Warren Buffett: "What the human being is best at doing is interpreting all new information so that their prior conclusions remain intact." News exacerbates this flaw. We become prone to overconfidence, take stupid risks and misjudge opportunities. It also exacerbates another cognitive error: the story bias. Our brains crave stories that "make sense" – even if they don't correspond to reality. Any journalist who writes, "The market moved because of X" or "the company went bankrupt because of Y" is an idiot. I am fed up with this cheap way of "explaining" the world.

News inhibits thinking. Thinking requires concentration. Concentration requires uninterrupted time. News pieces are specifically engineered to interrupt you. They are like viruses that steal attention for their own purposes. News makes us shallow thinkers. But it's worse than that. News severely affects memory. There are two types of memory. Long-range memory's capacity is nearly infinite, but working memory is limited to a certain amount of slippery data. The path from short-term to long-term memory is a choke-point in the brain, but anything you want to understand must pass through it. If this passageway is disrupted, nothing gets through. Because news disrupts concentration, it weakens comprehension. Online news has an even worse impact. In a 2001 study two scholars in Canada showed that comprehension declines as the number of hyperlinks in a document increases. Why? Because whenever a link appears, your brain has to at least make the choice not to click, which in itself is distracting. News is an intentional interruption system.

News works like a drug. As stories develop, we want to know how they continue. With hundreds of arbitrary story-lines in our heads, this craving is increasingly compelling and hard to ignore. Scientists used to think that the dense connections formed among the 100 billion neurons inside our skulls were largely fixed by the time we reached adulthood. Today we know that this is not the case. Nerve cells routinely break old connections and form new ones. The more news we consume, the more we exercise the neural circuits devoted to skimming and multitasking while ignoring those used for reading deeply and thinking with profound focus. Most news consumers – even if they used to be avid book readers – have lost the ability to absorb lengthy articles or books. After four, five pages they get tired, their concentration vanishes, they become restless. It's not because they got older or their schedules became more onerous. It's because the physical structure of their brains has changed.

News wastes time. If you read the newspaper for 15 minutes each morning, then check the news for 15 minutes during lunch and 15 minutes before you go to bed, then add five minutes here and there when you're at work, then count distraction and refocusing time, you will lose at least half a day every week. Information is no longer a scarce commodity. But attention is. You are not that irresponsible with your money, reputation or health. Why give away your mind?

News makes us passive. News stories are overwhelmingly about things you cannot influence. The daily repetition of news about things we can't act upon makes us passive. It grinds us down until we adopt a worldview that is pessimistic, desensitized, sarcastic and fatalistic. The scientific term is "learned helplessness". It's a bit of a stretch, but I would not be surprised if news consumption, at least partially contributes to the widespread disease of depression.

Social Media

Social Media

Social media can be too risque. It can be very impersonal and most important put you at risk for identity theft and make you a victim of circumstances. On Facebook a person can learn a lot about you. For instance, your spending habits, your marital status, your place of work, when your vacationing, where you hangout, where you live etc. I have two real life stories I will like to share with you. There was a couple attended my place of worship. They were excited about a trip they had been planning for a while. Not thinking they posted an update to their Facebook page when they were leaving and how long they would be gone. Assuming no harm was in informing family and friends of this much needed vacation, so their loved ones would know there whereabouts, they overlooked any potential threat in doing so. Well the day for their departure came, while the couple drove off into the sunset, some very caring neighbors took it upon themselves to move this couple out of there house, while they were away on vacation. The couple came back to an empty house and later discovered, that one of there good ole Facebook friends was the mastermind behind the whole ordeal.

The second story involves a lady from Nebraska. This lady was in her forties. She met a younger man online from Nigeria. They had dated online and everyone witnessed their love affair for two years. She was taking care of her live in mother who was sick and dying of cancer. So she was unable to travel outside the US to meet her suitor in person. From time to time she would send him money when he had asked. Due to his unfavorable conditions living in a third world country she just wanted to be of assistance. They were talking about the future and having children together and the whole nine yards. No one seemed suspicious of her Nigerian lover. One day she secretly gets a message on Facebook through her email. It was from another lady in Missouri, claiming to be his mistress. Through exchange of information, she had also been sending him money. Come to find out he was part of a group called the "yahoo boys" who pray on American women to lure them of their money. This young lady was duped out of her money, for lack of better words. However, unfortunately she learned a powerful lesson. Although social media is good for keeping in touch with, friends, family and some business ventures. It may not be wise to look for a mate. Now, I'm not completely saying that there is anything wrong with meeting a potential mate online. As a matter of fact many have. Even myself included have married from the internet. In the instance that you do decide to do such a thing, make sure you at least know one or two mutual friends. This puts more of a responsibility for the person to be on their P's and Q's. Not only that, it makes it harder for a person to hide who they really are. All things being equal, make sure that you more than get a chance to know the people that are closest to the person of said interest. These people will also bare the guilt of burden in the event that the online person happens to be a perpetrator. This was a sad outcome for the lady and it is unfortunate one at that. The moral of the two stories is to think of the major impact before you make commitments online or divulge information. Pro 14:15 The naive person believes every word, but the shrewd one ponders each step.

Vaccinations:

Again here is yet another topic that can be delivered with extreme coverage which would end up resulting in a book being produced on just this one topic alone. In the book "Healing Our Children" by Ramiel Nagel, there is a chapter in it

I absolutely love it's titled "Vaccinations Are Government-Sponsored Medical Bio terrorism and institutionalized Murder. In this chapter it covers a great variety of pieces to help plugin any unclear loopholes, leaving a thorough and clear understanding on the dangers of such treatment. Now sit and ponder on these words. Then ask yourself when has a vaccine eradicated the diseases in which we are led to believe we're seeking relief from? Again this is another destructive seed we have been led to sow in the minds of our children. We vaccinate them before their immune system even has a chance to grow.

We can also sow seeds of destruction when we think limiting thoughts or "stinking thinking." The way that we overcome this is by replacing it with positive ones instead. I have provided a list below of 8 patterns of destructive thinking. They are taken from the book Thoughts & Feelings by Matthew McKay, Martha Davis and Patrick Fanning. It is a fantastic book.

Eight Limited Thinking Patterns:

- **Filtering**—You focus on a negative detail while ignoring all the positive aspects of a situation

- **Polarized thinking**—Things are black or white, good or bad. You have to be perfect or you are a failure. There's no middle ground, no room for mistakes

- **Overgeneralization**—you reach a general conclusion based on a singular incident or piece of evidence. You exaggerate the frequency of problems and use negative global labels.

- **Mind Reading**—without their saying so, you know what people are feeling and why they act the way they act the way they do. In particular, you have certain knowledge of how people think and feel about you.

- **Catastrophizing**—You expect, even visualize disaster. You notice or hear about a problem and start asking, "What if?" What if tragedy strikes? What if it happens to you?

- **Magnifying**—You exaggerate the degree or intensity of a problem. You turn up the volume on anything bad, making it loud, large, and overwhelming.

- **Personalization**—You assume that everything people do or say is some kind of reaction to you. You also compare yourself to others, trying to determine who is smarter, more competent, better looking, more successful, and so on.

- **Shoulds**—You have a list of ironclad rules about how you and others should act. People who break the rules anger you and you feel guilty when you violate the rules.

The Neuroscience of Changing Harmful Thinking Patterns in a Relationship

The Neuroscience of Changing Harmful Thinking Patterns in Relationships:

It's truly astonishing when you consider it. You and your constitution are wired to cooperate to start neurochemical changes in your brain in the course of your most noteworthy great and happiness learned neural examples of considering, be that as it may, meddle with these regular driving forces.

Poisonous thinking is a protective strategy that unnecessarily activates the figure's survival reaction. Despite the fact that well intentions, basically, its an ineffective way of managing excruciating emotions, for example, not feeling "sufficient," meriting enough" or "having enough" in connection to others, all of which are a regular some piece of managing life or relationship issues, and different anxiety circumstances.

Taking into account later decades of neuroscience discoveries, it shows up, to the degree you get a conscious participant in these methods, you can all the more successfully run the progressions and parts of you included in change. As such, your accomplishment in changing any conduct or thought examples relies on upon ... cognizant you. [the issue here is ... that the vast majority of us have been adapted, by social convictions, mores, myths and conventions, in addition to everything else, to "think" in ways that make us genuinely question, abhor or gaze down our noses toward our "feeling self" (figure self, form mind and so forth.). This means our "wounded-personality self" rather than a "cognizant self" responsible for our overall astounding proficiencies (particular force) for creative ability, reflective considering, decision making - and when our wounded-conscience self is in control, contingent upon what triggers us, we're strolling around staying away from or evading the messages our figures send us about our minute by minute encounters in shifting degrees. We've confound our physique's indicators on the grounds that we take a gander at our feelings or others through the eyes of fear.]

As recommended to some degree. **1.** Your cerebrum and mind are a complex correspondence system, and what impacts change is a stream of information from a mix of sources, both cognizant and subconscious, hard- and delicate wired.

2. Data that is soft-wired has been learned, and in this manner could be unlearned or changed. Your contemplations and convictions fall in this classification; you have learned them, either deliberately or subconsciously, from the time you were initially laid open to language. in contrast, data that is hard-wired comprises of unalterable laws that represent the operation and life of your constitution, for example, inalienable heads to survive (physical and psychological self) and flourish (self in significant association).

This means you can change your delicate wiring (considerations, convictions, and so on), then again, any change should fundamentally happen inside a schema of unchangeable laws that govern how your cerebrum acclimates to change and certain angles of your nature as an individual.

You can change delicate soft-wired but not hard-wired information.

You can change data about you that is delicate wired, for example, old considerations and convictions and practices, then again, you can't change your hard-wiring. Case in point:

You can't change that your physique needs oxygen, nourishment and water to survive. you can't change that you additionally have an emotional psychological (spiritual?) drive to survive, i.e., to encounter your self as an one of a kind wellspring of thought, decisions, imaginative declaration, quality, commitment, thus on. You can't change that you are determined to seriously help in life and interface with life around you.

You can, in any case, change your musings and the principles or convictions that structure your contemplations.

Your benchmarks are situated by your constant considerations. Your contemplations reflect your convictions. Your activities are the best pointers of what you need and accept.

This guideline applies in every aspects of your life.

Your contemplations reflect your beliefs. They are your remarkable reactions to the occasions or persons throughout your life.

Your decisions reflect your musings. Your contemplations, by the level of substance "feel-great" sentiments they generate, impart what you need to your subconscious, and your passionate reactions convey what you outrageously need.

Your movements are the best pointers of your contemplations, needs and convictions. For example:

In the event that you don't have the relationship you need with your accomplice, it may be that you are centering excessively on their deficiencies, how unjustifiably they treat you, or some negative part of the relationship. This center, at any rate is part is supportive. Life is a first rate school and one of the discriminating lessons we all must take in (to be euphoric, savvy, satisfied and so forth.) is to treat each other with the poise we long for as an exchange.

The reaction we give or gain from others is excruciating, notwithstanding, all development enthusiastic, mental and physical much the same accompanies the standard of "no agony, no addition" or "utilization it, or lose it." the essential message you need your accomplice to comprehend is likely functional to them somehow, along these lines, the sentiment itself is all the more regularly not the issue. The issue is in how it is delivered and received, for example: It may be that the conveyance may be not exactly compelling. Assuming that you're set off when you convey your input, for instance, you're more inclined to utilize blame, fear- or disgrace prompting remarks, which thusly are likely to trigger your accomplice. The point when one or both of you are set off, your brains are in "defensive" instead of "taking in" mode, and subsequently blocking correspondence with an exhibit of tactics. It may likewise be the situation that, despite the fact that you're not upset when you convey your reaction, your accomplice gets set off the moment any indication of cynicism. Chances are that, when your accomplice gets activated and you don't get the reaction you required or needed i.e., comprehension, you're liable to get set off immediately too; accordingly once more, both of you are in "take out" modes — and your brains are immediately obstructing any messages from coming in or set out.

It's safe to say that an a major contribution to any incapable ways a partner convey or gain criticism comes from the restricting conviction framework they hold, for example, "If he/she adores me, they ought to realize what miracles me/what I need." Constraining convictions are connected with poisonous speculation examples, for example, "Affection ought not be work; I work 10 hour days and hope to have no requests on me at home." It is likewise the case that, over the long run, when an issue is not determined, our brains start to copartner "feel-terrible" sentiments with specific dialog or issues, or more regrettable, their mate may feel the same.. Conveyance and gaining of input is immediate as though emulating a script. Both "know" and advise themselves they're not going to get the effects they need, i.e., "Attempting to converse with him/her never lives up to expectations" or "I knew he/she couldn't do this without getting irate." In time, partners may set aside certain themes, or dodge circumstances, occasions, et cetera, so as to keep away from the feel-awful feelings. If you don't have the figure you need, it may be that you have solid emotions, i.e., fear or scorn, against some part of the techniques or activities that might provide for you the form you need. For instance, are you telling yourself that solid nourishments are "exhausting," or that you "love" certain garbage sustenances and couldn't in any way, shape or form live without them, or that you "fear" practice or "scorn" setting off to the rec center. Your subconscious's brain is listening 24/7, and like a genie satisfies your each wish as though it were a charge!

This reasoning, and the passionate states it generates, is ensured to keep you from arriving at your objectives. It's not in light of the fact that you are "disrupting" yourself or objectives, however it may feel that way. In truth, this is since your reasoning is not adjusted to your objectives. This means the objectives of your cognizant and subconscious personality are not in sync, which illustrates why you may not feel you have control of the course of your life.

You are dependably at the present time getting to be what you are most reasoning on the grounds that … your contemplations shape your movements.

You are always in the process of becoming what you are most thinking because … your thoughts shape your actions.

It might be said, you get to be your main event. What makes this uplifting news is that it implies you are in control of your feelings, activities and life more than you can envision (in present minutes). Your subconscious passes by what you outrageously need, and blazes and wires the neurons in your cerebrum likewise.

The issue is that sure decisions, which you have to be intentionally making, are, no doubt regulated by your subconscious.

You are hard-wired to seek feel-good products; avoid feel-bads.

The directives that legislate forms that immediately empower physical or enthusiastic feel-great or feel-terrible emotions in your physique are likewise unchangeable. They are joined with arrivals of hormones in the circulatory system that transform agreeable or frightful emotions accordingly. For illustration:

You can't control the directive that advises your subconscious to immediately dismiss from what causes sentiments of uneasiness or torment, and at the same time turn to what causes agreeable or feel-great feelings. you can't change that a few nourishments and substances immediately empower your faculties with feel-great emotions, could be addictive in nature, bring forth yearnings, and give just brief feel-goods. You can't change that your mind's capacity to "habituate" (in fusion with different capacities, for example, survival) permits you to get "acclimated" or adjust to even the most tormenting or unsafe practices and exercises.

Toxic thinking is harmful considering. These programmed intuition examples prepare the mind to arrive at for feel-merchandise for the purpose of feel-products, actually when they generally speaking make you (or others) feel terrible! Similarly as with other addictive or enthusiastic examples, this prepares your mind to look for the sort of feel-products that are fast and simple, despite the fact that they are pseudo feel-merchandise.

A fixation, you may say, is state of the psyche and form in which the mind gets restlessly centered, and progressively reliant, on an action or substance as a origin of solace. What gets lost when this happens is the capacity to live without dread and disgrace.

Emotions and feel-bads are there to show us and brief us.

They are sensations in the constitution – messages from your physique to you – that tell you where we are in connection to where we need to conceivably be. This is profitable data! To use this data, in any case, you need to know how to deal with your trepidation reaction to keep your brain and form cool enough to counteract your cerebrum from moving out of "taking in" into "defensive" mode.

Harmful supposing forestalls change. how?

Harmful feel-great examples are reasons or falsehoods we tell ourselves that are unbendingly held set up by dread, and that square us from seeing our own particular and other's potential. They:

Hold your mind in prepared position to effortlessly initiate your defensive protections. In survival mode, your subconscious personality permits no taking in, along these lines, no influence. Block your development, as keeps you attempting to encounter love with just a large portion of your heart. In request to impact coveted transform, you will need to get to know your subconscious. Reinforce an inflexible conviction that feelings of adoration and powerlessness are commonly exclusive. As such, your considerations are telling your subconscious that you "despise" frightful feelings, and you need to dispose of them, or "need to" evade them keeping in mind the end goal to feel "alright" about yourself. These methods you're summoning your subconscious personality to break hard-wired directives – which it can't and won't do! You are wired to battle with your reasons for alarm and vulnerabilities. It's the way you develop boldness and stretch to love with your entire heart. Keep you identifying with yourself and life around you from a cognitive-enthusiastic neural example you framed in the first years of your life, your early survival-love mechanism– especially when you feel pushed or set off.

Since restricting convictions and harmful thought examples can delude the energies of your psyche and form, its wise to retrain our thoughts and direct them to better thought patterns.

Guard Against Seeds of Deception

Guard Against Seeds of Deception

"Deception may give us what we want for the
present, but it will always take it away in the end"

-Rachel Hawthorne

"When one is in love, one always begins by deceiving
one's self, and one always ends by deceiving others.
That is what the world calls romance."

-Oscar Wilde

As you may notice, I started this chapter with two quotes. Reason being that this is a big deal. Deception, plays a large part in denial. Refusing to see the truth within ourselves and always seeing the deflection in others. If we are not honest with ourselves, we can never be honest with the next person. We should continuously have before us a affair with honesty. It should be an banquet spread out of truthfulness, filled with the sweet wine of honesty. The very essence of which we should be willing to build all of our foundations on. Truth should be the very fiber of which we are made of. We should be clothed in all it's glory and adornment. No groundwork has a lasting chance without truth as it's basis. In fact there is no justification for deception. Anything built on false premises will not last. The Substratum of the heart is not designed to contend with such a feat. It is not in the conscious of man to be deceptive. Deception is a skillful practice, to some it's even an art. Deception is whole in part a choice. A person can change the truth by changing the facts. However, the truth will always prevail. The saying proves true that what goes on in the dark always comes out in the light. More-so the frustrating thing is that more often than not, usually innocent people whined up getting hurt during the cross-fire.

Let's talk about "drugs" better known in our modern day society as medicine. The doctors endorse and regulate the "medications" by the millions to patients. Medications are found regarding idolatry worship and encouraged by it. They are medications of misdirection and enchantment and connected to idol worship. Pharmakeia (far-mak-i'- ah) is the Greek God of divination and witchcraft. Whenever you go to the drug store to get your medicine; recollect medications are a seed of misdirection that will entrance your brain. This is not by Divine Purpose, nor does it fit in Divine Order with God's Will. God has already given us herbs to indicate his forgiveness of mankind after the fall in Eden. The television has been used as a tool of deception. Our children are being exposed to the lie through the picture tube so there reasoning and perception can become delusional and twisted"""""""""" So their perceptive powers can become dulled. There are hidden sexual innuendos and spiritistic images. All in plain sight, these things are in front of our children eyes, playing on the mental screen of their minds. Instead we need to be feeding them a spiritual diet. Full of wholesome truths. God's Word has stood the test of time. This is the most translated and sold book worldwide. For what it is worth, it contains Ancient Wisdom. Most books that have been written, sprung off of the Bible anyways. We have all the things that we need to set us free from the deceptive powers of the mind. So **GIGO** *garbage in, garbage out* or **RIRO** rubbish in rubbish out.

We need to learn how to filter the mind. Never do we want to allow our conscious to become seared. To have a seared conscious is to not allow the truth to penetrate the figurative heart and mind. It will be wise on our part to start seeking truth. When deception takes root, it's powerful hold is hard to turn loose. Why do you think that when most people in a relationship, discover that the other person whom they thought the other person was, is revealed, they still stay? It is because from infancy we are told lies, by the people whom suppose to love us the most, our parents. From Santa Claus, Thee Tooth Fairy, to The Easter Bunny, we were led to believe in a reality that does not exist, mere fantasies. Now I'm starting to understand why ones think that God is a fairy-tale too. After all, you can't see him neither. However you can't see the wind, but you can see the manifestation of it. You know that electricity exists, but no one can explain the dynamics of how it comes into your home.

There is no logical way to try to understand anything spiritual about God through the five senses. The reason being is because God is a spirit and those worshiping him must worship him in spirit and truth. When we pray we go within. From within we are able to tap into another dimension, the spirit world. There God sits on his throne ready to hear your voice, waiting to answer. God is not a man and could never be. That is why we have a Mediator, Jesus Christ. Sorry, but God is the same today as he was yesterday, HE does not change. Man changes with the weather. Each circumstance, life changing event, career move etc changes the attitude of man. Yet God is not factored by time, nor is he a man that he shall tell a lie. As for man, depending on the nature of the situation he will determine rather to lie by omission, or be truthful. Sad thing is, sometimes people are only truthful if they see the benefit in it for them to do so. Furthermore, we are free moral agents, who have the gift of free will. The more we use it for good, the more you will reap in it's kind. There can never be a person that practices vile things to expect the highest good for his own soul. In fact, most individuals anticipate their own demise. It does not become a matter of if to them, it only becomes a matter of when?

In closing of this chapter remember that intentions are everything. Make sure that you do your utmost at all times to refrain from telling a lie. Even in cases where the truth may even hurt another individual. In the end it's better to be injured by the truth, than to be comforted with a lie. In Galatians 6:7-10 It starts by saying do not be deceived, second that God is one not to be mocked. Do you think that maybe God knew that there is a human tendency to deceive oneself? Of course, their is and if you think this then your reasoning is right.

Sowing Seeds of Peace

Sowing Seeds of Peace

Are you a Peacemaker or Pot-Stirrer?

The warming children' story of Jesus riding into Jerusalem on a donkey with palm branches waving isn't as awesome as it may appear. We perceive the moment to be loaded with grins and festival, both from Jesus, his pupils, and the basic individuals, however this is not the truth of what happened.

The good news of Luke helps carry this actuality to life: "As he approached Jerusalem and saw the city, he sobbed over it and said, 'Assuming that you, even you, had just known on this day what might carry you peace—but now it is avoided your eyes'" (19:41-42). Jesus sobbed. He wasn't grinning or praising, he was overcome with distress in light of the fact that he knew his passing was nearing, he saw what's to come pulverization of the blessed city, and he knew the individuals were searching for a warrior lord instead of a peace-production ruler.

The yells from the crowd rang out, "Hosanna!" This is not a celebratory word, yet a sob for awesome benevolence. The individuals thought Jesus was coming to lead a war against the Roman government, so they were shouting out Hosanna, which signifies "spare us, we ask." But Jesus' triumphant section was such a great amount of more than that.

He entered Jerusalem demonstrating a lifestyle of peacemaking, not of war. He entered the heavenly kingdom considering you, of what's to come for his kingdom, and the sacrifice he needed to make with a specific end goal to get it going. He was not a war ruler, yet rather a child of God ready to surrender everything to unite his father's creation.

We battle with the thought of making peace in little ways today. On a huge scale with issues like prejudice, wrongdoing, characteristic fiasco, and world wars we'll hop to roads to dissent peace and bounce on twitter to request justice; they are deserving of our consideration and deliberations.

Anyway in our regular world where we run into smaller interruptions of peace we give them a chance to pass by without a second look. We get aloof and desensitized.

The boisterous mouth child tormenting, pugnacious worker at work, rude client hassling, companion that dependably differs and words sting, all the pot-stirrers in life who always need to make a disturbance to like themselves—all little minutes we essentially permit to happen time and again. Bear in mind about your disasters, as well. The cases where you overcompensate or turn into a touch of unfriendly, where you personally engage in war instead of living out peace.

In the event that we long to be more Christ-like, maybe restricted we could do it is by turning off the high temperature and taking without end the spoon of the pot-stirrers by sowing seeds of peace. No compelling reason to take up arms or get threatening, simply carry peace, "for he himself is our peace" (Ephesians 2:14a).

Going Deeper:how might you be able to accumulate peace in your life? Are there minutes you have neglected by where you could have sowed Christ-like peace, or minutes you responded with unfriendliness where you ought to have been? These are great questions for all of us to reflect and ponder over. We should be able to answer these self inquiries with true honesty. Allowing opportunity for new seeds to be produced. The more you sow according to God he will multiply it plenty. Who doesn't want an abundance of peace?

"Seek peace and pursue it"

~Hebrews 12:14

Reader:

I asked God if that made me a hypocrite. This led me to James 3; 18 now my understanding here is that hypocrisy comes when we "pretend" to do something. I did not't pretend to sow the seeds in peace; I actually sowed seeds in peace. I did not't fake this peace, I want this peace, but none the less I did not "feel" the peace in my heart. Does this mean that I want see the reality of the peace I seek, in my situation?

Reply:

What does it intend to "make" peace? The saying making is an activity, it intends to create or advance. Peace doesn't simply happen; we "get" it going. We do this when we decide to ignore the sins of others, we do this when we decide to pardon, and we do this when we decide to make the best choice actually when it doesn't "feel" right to our spirit.

Reader:

I inquired as to whether that made me a faker. This headed me to James 3; now my seeing here is that deception comes when we "pretend" to do something. I didn't claim to sow the seeds in peace; I really sowed seeds in peace. I didn't fake this peace, I need this peace, however none the less I didn't" "feel" the peace in my heart.

Reply:

It's hard for somebody to be scornful to you when you accompany an olive branch extension. I know all excessively well what it is to "make" peace, not "feel" peace. It's hard, one of the hardest things that I have ever needed to do. I am an individual who has faith in equity and responsibility. Here and there this impedes making peace for me. I don't reason that I have all or even a small amount of the answers. What I do know is that regardless of the possibility that if I don't "feel" at peace with the seeds that I am sowing; I am making the best decision on the grounds that I am not emulating my own flesh, yet rather I am taking after the example that Jesus left for me. The bible says "seek peace and pursue it." The word pursue means to carry on a course of action or train of thought. If you train you mind that peace is the end result in which you you are striving after, it will just be a matter of time before you feel it in your heart as well. The result that we are searching for when we sow seeds for God is uprightness. We know this on the grounds that is the thing that this verse says. It lets us know what the "products of the soil" of the seed is. How are we to "sow" the seed? In peace. What's more in what capacity would we be able to do that? By "making" peace or to seek peace and pursue it.

Sowing Seeds of Blessings

Sowing Seeds of Blessings

Tragically people grow up in families and never receive a blessing or live with a marriage partner but never feel their approval or go through an entire school year and not feel accepted by teachers or, even worse, their peers.

Everyone wants and needs a blessing. An Old Testament story illustrates this quite well. Isaac had two sons, Esau and Jacob. Nearing the end of his life, Isaac wanted to give his blessing to his oldest son, Esau. But Jacob, through the conniving of his mother, tricked Isaac into giving him the blessing that was intended for Esau. When Esau heard that his father had blessed Jacob, "He cried out with a loud and bitter cry and said to his father, "Bless me—me too, my father! . . . Isn't he rightly named Jacob? For he has cheated me twice now. He took my birthright, and look, now he has taken my blessing.' Then he asked, 'Haven't you saved a blessing for me?' . . . 'Do you only have one blessing, my father? Bless me—me too, my father!' And Esau wept loudly'" (Gen. 27:34, 36, 38).

There is not enough emphasis in my words to properly communicate what was in Esau's voice when he said, "Bless me too, my father." This is the cry of every child to his or her parents. This is the cry of every spouse to his or her mate. This was the cry of boy and girl the cry of every woman or man. This is the cry of people you rub shoulders with every day. It may even be your cry.

Genuine acceptance is an unmet need in so many people today, but it does not have to be that way. You can give a blessing to those people. Here's how.

I. A blessing needs to be felt

In the Scriptures, touch played an important part in the bestowal of the family blessing. When Isaac blessed Jacob, an embrace and a kiss were involved. The same is true today. We want and, often, need to feel the embrace of those we love.

It's an old story, but its truth transcends to time now. A little four-year-old girl became frightened late one night during a thunderstorm. After one particularly loud clap of thunder, she jumped up from her bed, ran down the hall, and burst into her parent's room. Jumping right in the middle of the bed, she sought out her parent's arms for comfort and reassurance. "Don't worry, honey," her father said, trying to calm her fears. "The Lord will protect you."

The little girl snuggled closer to her father and said, "I know that, Daddy, but right now I need someone with skin on!"

This little girl did not doubt her heavenly Father's ability to protect her, but she was also aware that he had given her an earthly father she could run to: someone whom God had entrusted with a special gift that could bring her comfort, security, and personal acceptance—the blessing of meaningful touch.

As a teenager, I desperately wanted to please my older brother. Kerry has a unique way of making people feel special. He is a bit different, but extremely a gentleman. Through my adolescence he was the best friend I every had, I vividly recall the times I would be in the house alone and he would come and take me with him to play outside. Instead of scolding me, he would place his enveloping hand on my shoulder, and explain my mistake, and then offer instruction for improvement. His touch communicated acceptance in spite of disappointment, no matter what it was.

Have you ever noticed how often the Biblical writers speak of Jesus touching people? He touched the sick, the lepers, the blind, the deaf, the prostitutes, the outcasts. A tender moment in the life of Christ was when the children came to him. "Some people were bringing little children to him so he might touch them, but his disciples rebuked them. When Jesus saw it, He was indignant and said to them, "Let the little children come to me. Don't stop them, for the kingdom of God belongs to such as these. I assure you: Whoever does not welcome the kingdom of God like a little child will never enter it." After taking them in his arms, he laid His hands on them and blessed them." (Mark 10:13-16). Jesus modeled for us the communication of a blessing through touch.

Never stop giving meaningful touches. Hugs, holding hands, the stroke of a head, and the arm around a shoulder all communicate acceptance, approval, importance and value. To neglect meaningful touch is to fail to transmit the blessing to others.

II. A blessing needs to be spoken

In the Scriptures the family blessing hinged, also, on a spoken message. Abraham spoke a blessing to Isaac. Isaac spoke it to his son Jacob. "When Isaac smelled his clothes, he blessed him and said . . ." (Gen. 27:27). Jacob spoke it to each of his twelve sons and to two of his grandchildren. You see, a blessing is not a blessing unless it is spoken.

I have had constant affirmations. I needed those words then. I still need them now. Great power is incarnated in words. "Life and death are in the power of the tongue, and those who love it will eat its fruit" (Prov. 18:21). Words have the incredible power to build us up or tear us down. The saying, "Sticks and stones may break my bones, but words will never hurt me," is an absolute lie. Words have the power of death. They inflict pain. They can destroy a friendship, rip apart a home, or cause harm in a marriage. And when these harmful words are spoken, it is almost impossible to call them back.

Yet, on the other hand, words have the undeniable power to build people up. Words can be the source of healing, forgiveness, and life. Our children, our spouse, our friends, our work mates—everyone we rub shoulders with—long to hear words of approval, acceptance, and affection. And, let me add, they need to hear those words before and after they have made a mistake or gotten into trouble. With the spoken blessing, we express the value and worth of the individual. Believe me, everyone you know longs to hear such phrases as, "I love you." "You are important to me." "You are going to make a difference in this world one day."

Begin today, communicating your blessing to others. Especially your children, if you have them. One great tragedy in life is that we wait until it is too late to say how we feel about people we love. We will travel miles for a funeral to visit the dead before we go around the corner to visit someone alive and well. The Scriptures say, "When it is in your power, don't withhold good from the one to whom it is due. Don't say to your neighbor, 'Go away! Come back later. I'll give it tomorrow'—when it is there with you" (Prov. 3:27-28). Have you ever been to a family reunion? For most of the time people will talk about sports, recipes, movies, or the latest news events. But something happens the last hour of the reunion. Suddenly, before the family members say their good-byes, meaningful words will be spoken. A brother will say in private to his sister, "I know things will work out in your marriage. I'll be praying for you." An aunt will say to her niece, "You've always made me proud. I know school is hard, but you can do it. I believe in you." Or a daughter will say to a mother, "Look around you, Mom. We didn't turn out half bad, did we? We have you and Dad to thank." So often the most meaningful words are said just before the good-byes. Sometimes when we wait, we wait too long. And those words we wanted to say, or wanted to hear, are lost forever.

III. A blessing attaches special value to the person

When we value something we place great importance on it. This is at the heart of the concept of blessing. In Hebrew, to "bow the knee" is the root meaning of blessing. This root word is used of a man who has his camel bend his knee so he could get on. In relationship to God the word came to mean "to adore with bended knees." Bowing before someone is a graphic picture of valuing that person. Anytime we bless someone, we are attaching high value to him or her.

Isaac placed great value on Jacob when he blessed him. He said, "So he came closer and kissed him. When Isaac smelled his clothes, he blessed him and said: 'Ah, the smell of my son is like the smell of a field that the LORD has blessed. May God give to you—from the dew of the sky and from the richness of the land—an abundance of grain and new wine. May peoples serve you and nations bow down to you. Be master over your brothers; may your mother's sons bow down to you. Those who curse you will be cursed, and those who bless you will be blessed" (Gen. 27:27-29). When Isaac told Jacob he smelled like a field he was communicating to his son that he was as refreshing as a newly cut field of hay or wheat. These were words of value to Jacob. First, Isaac was painting a picture for his son that one day other people would bow down to him. Second, it was a reminder that we would be a man of great respect because he was valuable. We can't miss the idea in these two pictures of praise that Jacob's father thought he was very valuable, someone who had great worth.

To express words of high value in some people we don't have to look very deep or very far. But for others it means that sometimes we must dig deep to discover the value of that individual. Sometimes it means that we must see what others do not see. We must see their potential and point it out to that individual. I love Michelangelo's response to the question, "How do you sculpture such beautiful angels?" He replied, "I see the angel in the marble and chisel until I set it free." That is what we must do with some people. We must look beyond the surface. We must point out a person's worth and value, and in doing so, we have the power to set them free. That's giving a blessing.

This is what Jesus did for Peter. Peter was called Simon before Jesus entered his life. Simon was a rough and tough fisherman who was unstable and insecure. Jesus came along and called him Peter, or Rock, and those words changed his life. Before, he was more like shifting sand. But one word or hope and Jesus pointed out his value created a man as strong and stable as a rock.

You can turn someone's life around by giving them a blessing. Through meaningful touch, a spoken word, and pointing out their value. Believe it or not you have the power to change the direction of someone's life.

Conclusion

Perhaps you have come to adulthood and don't feel blessed. Your parents may never be able to bless you, but there is a heavenly Father anxious to bless you. You don't have to come, like Jacob and Esau deceiving God, pretending you are someone else. You can come just like you are, feeling inadequate or like a failure, knowing you are a sinner, and God will love you, forgive you, and accept you, and make you his child and bless you. The story of Jesus Christ is one way how God touches us and communicates his blessing to us.

Sowing Seeds of Forgiveness

Sowing Seeds of Forgiveness

"Tony Robbins - Forgiveness is a gift you give yourself.."

It will be wise to note that forgiveness is for you and not the other person. The Bible tells us to forgive others as God has forgiven you. To hold a grudge against someone keeps you in bondage and makes you a slave to the other individual. By letting go, you in a sense free yourself of the other person's power over you. Many health concerns and illnesses springs forth from harboring resentment, which stems from not forgiving. Most hidden behavioral problems lie in the unsettlement of issues. When we choose not to forgive we allow ourselves to close the door to prayer. No matter how many that we send up on a daily basis, if we haven't forgiving a person in our heart, then our prayers go no further than the ceiling. Jesus gives us the secret to a more abundant life at Matthew 6:14. Here we learn that in order for our errors to be pardoned, we have to pardon others who sin against us.

If God intended for us to live in the past he would have plastered eyes in the back of our head. Since this is not't the case, it would be wise to look ahead for what the future holds, instead of holding on to the past. I'm not saying to never reflect. Reflection, from time to time is good. In fact this is how we grow. However, it's one thing to reflect on the past and quite another to vacation there. Let alone move back there, and leave the present moment to chance. We all fall victim to circumstance. Each and everyone of us has also offended others, rather in words or deeds. We're not above reproach. With that being said, let's keep a level mind and do not become pretentious or haughty. I presume that we all have fallacies and we are not perfect. So it will not be fair to uphold someone to high standards that are even out of your own reach.

Sowing Seeds of Joy

Sowing Seeds of Joy

"Those who sow with tears will reap with songs of joy."

Psalms 126:5

Joy like any other altitude can come and go. We are not guaranteed joy just because we are believers. More is actually involved. I will explain how you can have lasting joy amidst, your current situation in life, in further detail later in this chapter. For some, joy can be fleeting or temporary. Therefore we must locate or surround ourselves of constant experiences of possible joys. Be gathered with individuals who celebrate the very person that you are. Not with those who want to box you and secretly turn you into carbon copies of themselves, personally adopting you as one of their "little mini me's." In our own individuality we can find our true source of gumption, ambitions, desires and what sets us apart and makes us individually stand out.

Joy is a choice, it is a decision that you make that come what may, you are determined to stay in the "secret hiding place of Jehovah." In that place no one can steal your joy, because joy abounds all around you. Look up in the sky, what do you see? Look into the field, the garden, the streets you roam about. Hear the childrens' laughter. Take a deep breath, as you do, feel your lungs fill up with air. In this very moment as you exhale, feel the weight on your heart be released with your exhalation. Not for one moment did you ever wonder if your next breath of air was going to come or not. Joy is what you are therefore seeking.... but yet and still it's all around you. If you can't see it with your physical eyes, how are you going to perceive with your spiritual senses. Start where you are planted first, then God will excel you to newer higher and heights. If you so as much can't start here, ask for a sense of direction in prayer. If you fail to do this joy will always elude you.

Jehovah is a happy God. To give you joy makes HIM joyous. He is also generous and kind and gives freely. If you ask for joy in abundance, then in the name of Jesus it's YES and Amen. The bible says you have not because you ask not. You have joy in great volumes. Myriads and myriads of joy is all around you in that place. The very secret hiding place of Jehovah. No one can penetrate your contentment or enter into your inner sanctum or sanctuary. For you yourself would have a circle formed around about you, for only you and your Creator. That you have personally formed by your bond with HIM. HIM in whom is shaping and molding the very person you are. Whom is refining you like fine gold and removing the dross off of your very being. This ONE yes the Grand Creator who created all things has entertained you day and night to the ambiance of sweet melody of joy with laughter as it's kinsmen and happiness as it's lodging place. Reclining together in the bosom position of his undeserved kindness. There was nothing we ever had to do to get here, but except Jesus invitation to come be his follower. We are certainly privileged to serve such an awesome God such as Jehovah.

Sowing Seeds of Happiness

Sowing Seeds of Happiness

"The law of harvest is to reap more than you sow. Sow an act, and you reap a habit. Sow a habit and you reap a character. Sow a character and you reap a destiny."

-James Allen

First, you start by uprooting negativity, or anything that resembles unhappiness. It all starts with thought. We must learn to look our fears, weariness, and anxiety directly in the eye, and instead of seeing what is impossible according to the eyes, we need to go within and start perceiving from the invisible, which we cannot see. You can do this by doing spiritual work. Inside of ourselves we may find a lot of work that needs to be done. The reward is rising above the inner limitations. No doubt everyday life may try to get the best of us. All of us have self-limiting thoughts. Often times we find that we can be our own worst enemy. There are even times that we may self-sabotage. Cast your fears aside, because God is the majority in every problem. Happiness, you see is an inside job. We cannot look to external sources for true happiness.

If you knew that you had at your disposal a helper that was qualified to accomplish any task, answer any questions, no limitations to physical circumstances and will never get sick or never sleep and you had access to this person 24/7. If all you had to do is accept him to go work for you immediately and put faith in him that he would never fail you. Would you accept this role from the aforementioned person? Remember the only requirement was to have unfailing faith that he will never fail you. You had to follow a few safety rules to protect you, not him, from life's woes. The best part is it is at no cost to you, yet it will yield you time and time again, un estimated values. These values ranges in there quality and quantity. They can come randomly in spurts, droves, access or in direct proportion of what you give out. Be it good or bad you will reap it's kind. Would not you want to reap a bountiful harvest? Despite the tendency to do wrong, if you knew that you had this law working for you 24/7 hours..... 365 days a week, would you not be willing to be a companion to such as person? I think you get the gist of what it is I'm trying to convey. The relationship is with your Heavenly Father. No matter what he will never leave you nor forsake you. We always look for happiness but fail to realize you are empowered to be happy or sad, it's a choice most importantly your choice.

Our beliefs are instilled in us from birth, many of them are false and no longer serve us. Holding on to these ideas can have a great impact on the way that we think and act in certain situations. It can be a conundrum to how we respond and to our fears. Some individuals fear happiness because they feel that something is lurking in the background to go wrong. But what we fear, may never come upon us. The very thing that we dread may not ever happen, but still we carry this unhealthy fear. Others fear that they will never be happy because the feel they are undeserving. Yet still we are all under Jehovah's undeserving loving kindness. We have two choices in life. Either we can see the good in what life has to offer, or we can see the bad, in which will take from us. In healing from past hurts, it is of vital importance that we let everything go that does not serve the current status in your life. In a book by Joseph Murphy, it gives practical steps in healing through prayer. "The first step in healing is not to be afraid of the manifest condition — from this very moment. The second step is to realize that the condition is only the product of past thinking, which will have no more power to continue its existence. The third step is mentally to exalt the miraculous healing power of God within you. This procedure instantly will stop the production of all mental poisons in you or in the person for whom you are praying. Live in the embodiment of your desire, and your thought and feeling will soon be made manifest. Do not allow yourself to be swayed by human opinion and worldly fears, but live emotionally in the belief that it is God in action in your mind and body."

In this lifetime there are many that are on the pursuit of happiness, however it is within everyone's reach. It is true that what you are seeking is seeking you. Happiness requires cooperation. Most importantly it takes time. At the seat of the soul, it is there for the taking, but requires work. Each day we have to plant seeds of positive thinking, and happiness will be the fruits from the seedlings. Day by day, night by night, we have to water it and make it grow. Beyond the shadow of doubt, we have to know, that what is true of God is true of us too. He is a happy God sitting on his throne, says the book of Job. Most certainly he wants us to be happy too. Happiness will not elude the mind that has already toiled and prepared the mind of the worker. Whereas for the one who is lazy and conservative in heart and sprit, happiness will always escape him/her. Long live the days where we seek for things that are not there. What you give is positively what you get. So if it's happiness that you seek, than happiness is what you get. Just like if you want more love, then give it. If you want more money give it without expectation of receiving and so forth. Unquestionably, if all your undertakings a done in the right attitude and spirit of mind, then as a byproduct the happiness that you seek in in the inner chambers. There in this place is the unlimited supply of abundance of happiness. Visualize this everyday. Think of a happy place and treat it as your passport to escape everyday stress. You will find not only happiness, but peace of mind. Do it this way for about 5 minutes one day. Then 10 minutes the next, adding five extra minutes a day, until you are at least at 30 minutes everyday. The longer you stay in this happy place the quicker you will see the manifestation of your happiness, start to unfold.

Sowing Seeds of Health

Sowing Seeds of Health

"He that has health has hope, and he that has hope has everything."

-Arabian Proverb

What we ingest or put into our body will either heal or kill us. You are either feeding the disease or fighting it with healing foods. Some have been led to believe that eating healthy is just a scheme to dupe you for more money. But in reality, you should be asking yourself, why is the food that is harmful cost less? To answer this it is filled with chemical fillers and carcinogenic substances. No one is educated enough or has a Chemist degree to figure out that the ingredients listed is filled with unstable, non human consumption, forbidden by God himself pseudo-foods. Pseudo-meaning fake, undigestible, take you to your grave early food. If it can last on a shelf for years without rotting, then what will your stomach acid do, up against such a daunting task as enzyme deprived food? Enzymes are essential to life, with out them we will die. Where there are no enzymes, there is no life, period! Can you imagine how many pounds of undigested food the average American has each year, in their intestinal tract? Let's face it our "sewer system" the "colon" is backed the heck up! If the average person can carry 22 lbs of undigested food in there colon, then what about those that are obese? Now your reels are starting to churn huh?

I cannot imagine how we can expect health when our internal plumbing is a breeding ground for bad bacteria and putrefaction. We should have implemented into our diets a health management and maintenance program. This entails of the cleaning of our colon through an enema at least once a week minimum. Then we need to cleanse the liver every six months. Along with the liver we should, flush the kidneys and the gall bladder needs cleansing as well. We need to fast at least once a week. Now that would be idea for the average person, but what about the sick person? Well for all chronic illnesses, at least 2 colonics a day minimum. You can do even up to three to four if need be. Just using plain water. No additives unless your doing a Wheatgrass or Probiotic Implant. The secret to health is to keep the first lines of our of defense, our immunity unclog, which starts in the gut. All illnesses or dis-ease starts in the gut. If you are fighting any battle, start here first. Dr. Kellogg estimated that over 90% of the "diseases of civilization" were due to a blocked and non-functioning colon.

– cited in Iridology: the Science and Practice p 408.

Here's a 60 day program that is effective in eradicating dis-ease:

Build up the flora, begin a cleansing diet, and restore normal digestion and effortless elimination. No magic bullets here; for 60 days we need:

THE PROGRAM

60 DAYS
1. Affix NEOL Spa Diet to refrigerator door, with magnet, in a location of maximum guilt potential.
2. No dairy: pasteurized milk, cheese, butter, yogurt, white dressings, creamy soups, ice cream.
3. No REFINED sugar: cookies, donuts, soft drinks, candy, junk, and desserts
4. Eat in MODERATION, but from the NEOL Spa Diet. Never be hungry.
5. Drink 2 liters of water per day (not tap water).
6. Three whole food enzymes caps, three times a day. (**All-Zyme)
7. First 60 days: 1 dropperful first day,1 1/2 dropperful on 2nd day, day 3 take 2 dropperfuls all the way to day 7, then break a day and proceed until week three, taking 2 dropperfuls twice a day. Go for max. (e.g., *Genesis Today Liquid Cleanser Take as directed if you're relatively a healthy person. (blends, e.g. Saccharomyces Boulardii+MOS, not single species — see Products)
9. Consider stopping all drugs, both prescription and over the counter
10. Get the lumbar spine adjusted. or N.E.A.T. Technique, Natural Energy Alignment Technique.

That's it. A 60-day colon detox. Doing part of it or your own version of it is a waste of time. It's a unit.

What is N.E.A.T?

Everyone can benefit from N.E.A.T. and many people are! Holistic healing involves the healing of the mind, body, and spirit. Emotions affects us all, no matter what we have to deal with them, or they will cause disease. N.E.A.T. is a holistic technique that provides benefits physically, mentally, and spiritually. Perhaps you have been faithful to your nutritional program, taking your supplements regularly, drinking plenty of pure water, eating all the right foods for your body chemistry, exercising, yet you still don't feel quite well, like something is missing. N.E.A.T. can be your answer to complete your holistic wellness program.

This is a true concept that we live or die on a cellular level. However, I'm going to take it even deeper:

> Just as we physically live and grow by the food of the
> earth that God has given us, we must spiritually live and
> grow by the food of heaven that God has given us. There is
> no other way to physically live and grow, and there is no
> other way to spiritually live and grow. If we refuse or neglect
> to eat physical food, we physically die, and if we refuse or
> neglect to eat spiritual food, we spiritually die. To try to
> spiritually live and grow without the spiritual food God
> has given us makes as much sense as trying to live and grow
> without the physical food God has given us. Neither is
> possible. It's as simple and direct as that.

There are three immune systems; physical, emotional and spiritual. Each level has it's on effects. I decided to talk about this in my next book for the sake of staying in context with the current subject matter. This book goes a lot deeper into the spiritual laws of the Universe and reaching out to connect to the Creator, in such a way that you will feel HIS every presence with you each day. If we feel his spirit in every cell of your body, you could never get sick. It's not a miracle to be well, it's your birthright. More often than not we call a doctor first when we fall sick, before we call the one keeping watch over our souls. Most importantly who knows the direct cause and the solution better than the one in whom created you? Not to discredit doctors, for I am such, but God is the healer! All other things have there place, never put them in God's position though. Just as there is no virtue in poverty, there is no reward in sickness. To be an invalid or infirmed does not gain you undue mercies with God. You can't bargain your way into the kingdom of the heavens, no more than a sinner asking God for a bribe! The enemy well knows that to be whole you have to be well in all facets of life. Their is a great balancing act that needs to be had when it comes to well being. Nature is not stupid, for what goes wrong in nature, nature knows how to take care of it.

What you put into the body is manifested in either good or poor health. Never be mistaken that you can eat whatever you want and the body will obey your demand for health. Not a single cell will respond favorably without having the right conditions conducive to good health. The reason that diet do not work is because it only works on the physical level and forfeits the other two. Your conditioning of your mind will either make you stay true to form or make you question you very existence. Gather yourself for the spiritual journey first and all these other things will fall into play.

Sowing Seeds of Wealth

Sowing Seeds of Wealth

A simple rule of building riches is to think freely, free of impact from the masses. Thinking autonomously begins with grasping the eccentric, and settling on choices for the better of your money related future, not dependent upon what social order esteems as typical or adequate. It bodes well that just 3% of the population is a 'high net earner" single person. As far as I can tell most of the 97% are simply indiscreetly using, keeping up with the Jones, or the Kardashians' and arriving at for affirmation and acknowledgment at any liability. Sadly, most of the population have a large portion of their choices managed by promoting, relatives, companions and social order. I call this in particular tyranny. Be conscious, in the event that you use cash frequently on attire, devices, collectibles, and at upper scale restaurants, its difficult to accumulate riches in the event that you're spending before you earn.

Thinking legitimately, to be in the 3%, its sensible to surmise that you must be wildly unpredictable, be a independent thinker, go against regular societal practices and be ready to do whatever is required to attain your riches building objectives, else you'll be much the same as the vast majority of the 97%. Stay away from individual fascism. However, make sure whatever you do you are being ethical and honest.

In the event that you're poor beginning off on small means, you need to abatement your month to month expenditures in a true and objective way. In the event that you are simply scraping by to pay your rent every month, its essentially difficult to have a significant rich building arrangement. Understanding this and making true progressions is a vital venture to storing up riches. My consultation is to move in with roommates, or move to a neighborhood in a more seasoned piece of town where rent is more reasonable. Particularly assuming that you're expecting a yield from the fruits of your labor, exorbitant living is not a necessity from a fortune building viewpoint. Different approaches to reduction your altered costs are to search for better arrangements on auto protection, cease your landline telephone, purchase an used vehicle and eat healthier. Less cash for settled overheads provides for you more to put resources into your riches building arrangement.

Recognizing and regulating your bad habit might be a main variable when building fortune. For the most part, the measure of cash used to help an individual's bad habit can undoubtedly supplement a fruitful fortune building arrangement. Basic issues could be drugs, liquor, shopping, overspending and so forth. Facing these tests is the first venture, than it takes free thinking to make the progressions required to carry on with a more fortune arranged lifestyle. In that lays the hardest part for some piece of building fortune, really making the extreme, disagreeable choice that most individuals might keep away from, and perseveringly adhering to it over your riches building journey

Contacting a banking intuition is a point worth underscoring, then again, brokerage group contribution and societal practices with free and free thinking is the most powerful riches building consolidation of all. Small time can achieve next to no compared to what a gathering of similar men who cooperate can finish. Be conscious that societal interaction has its allurements and it might be not difficult to forsake cheapness and independence. combining freedom and independence, while leveraging social interaction is a robust establishment for a fortune building arrangement. This is the place individuals require the most discipline.

Preferably, assuming that you can tweak your lifestyle and be reliable, you can spare a heap of cash by industriously polishing the above standards.

That is the critical issue; the simple part is the real contributing. Basically put the cash you spare in a generally held stock record finance consistently (you can discover these through your bank or firm). Rehash every month. hold till budgetary opportunities your bank or firm). Rehash every month. hold till budgetary opportunities are realized and you are stable enough through your stock indexes.

Sowing Seeds of Abundance

Sowing Seeds of Abundance

In the same way that seeds flourish in the soil and develop and presents to its own particular harvest, so it is with the individuals who offer fiscally to God. The Ruler is capable to duplicate the seed given and return it once more to the supplier. The Ruler Jesus proclaims in Luke 6:38 "Give, and it ought be given unto you; great measure, pressed down, and shaken together, and running over, might men give into your chest. For with the same measure that ye distribute withal it ought be measured to you once more." In the event that we put our cash in banks and we gain the little interest that we do, then what amount more will God reproduce our seed for being respectful to His Pledge and giving brightly from our hearts? The Lord Jehovah even provokes us to give with the goal that we can perceive how unwavering He truly is. We read in Malachi 3:10 "Carry ye all the tithes into the storage facility, that there may be meat in mine house, and demonstrate me now herewith, saith the Jehovah of armies, in the event that I won't open you the windows of paradise, and pour you out a gift, that there might not be room enough to gain.

What we must remember is that everything begins with the seed. Whether it is a plant, a food or a human being, it all started with a seed. Before a farmer can harvest his fruits, vegetables or grains, he must first plant the appropriate seeds that will give him the harvest he needs. Then he must be diligent to fertilize, water and watch over his seeds to make sure they are healthy and growing in order to finally bring him his harvest. So it is with us. We are to sow our seeds with diligence and keep them watered with our prayers so when our harvest comes in, it will be well worth our wait.

Planting Seeds in Your Children

Planting Seeds in Your Children

Our Children—A Precious Inheritance

"Look! Sons are an inheritance from Jehovah; the fruitage of the belly is a reward."—PSALM 127:3.

CONSIDER the miraculous events that Jehovah God made possible by the way he created the first man and woman. Both the father, Adam, and the mother, Eve, contributed a part of themselves that developed within Eve's womb into a fully formed new person—the first human baby. (Genesis 4:1) Down till today, the conception and birth of a child fill us with wonder and are described by many as nothing short of a miracle.

Within some 270 days, the original cell that was created within the mother as a result of her union with the father grows into a baby made up of trillions of cells. That original cell has within it the instructions needed to produce more than 200 kinds of cells. Following those marvelous instructions, which are beyond human understanding, these cells of stunning complexity develop in just the right order and manner to form a new living person!

Who, would you say, is the real maker of the baby? It is surely the One who created life in the first place. The Bible psalmist sang: "Know that Jehovah is God. It is he that has made us, and not we ourselves." (Psalm 100:3) Parents, you well know that it is not because of any brilliance on your part that you have produced such a precious little bundle of life. Only a God of infinite wisdom could be responsible for the miraculous formation of a new living human. For thousands of years, reasoning people have credited the formation of a child inside its mother's womb to the Grand Creator. Do you?—Psalm 139:13-16.

Is Jehovah, though, an unfeeling Creator who simply instituted a biological process whereby men and women could produce offspring? Some humans are unfeeling, but Jehovah is never like that. (Psalm 78:38-40)

The Bible says at Psalm 127:3: "Look! Sons [and daughters as well] are an inheritance from Jehovah; the fruitage of the belly is a reward." Let us now consider what an inheritance is and what it gives evidence of.

An inheritance is like a gift. Parents often work long and hard to leave their children an inheritance. It may consist of money, property, or perhaps some treasured possession. In any case, it is evidence of a parent's love. The Bible says that God has given parents their children as an inheritance. They are a loving gift from him. If you are a parent, would you say that your actions show that you view your little ones as a gift that the Creator of the universe has entrusted to you?

Jehovah's purpose in granting this gift was to have the earth populated with the descendants of Adam and Eve. (Genesis 1:27, 28; Isaiah 45:18) Jehovah did not individually create every human, as he did the millions of angels. (Psalm 104:4; Revelation 4:11) Instead, God chose to create humans with the ability to produce children who would resemble their parents in identifiable ways. What a marvelous privilege it is for a mother and father to bring forth and care for such a new person! As parents, do you thank Jehovah for making it possible for you to enjoy this precious inheritance?

Numerous days I fear. I alarm myself many times over about coming up short before them. My shortcomings may overpower me here and there. I only have this one opportunity to develop them and I need to get it right. I'll supplicate that the God might lead me in heading them. I supplicate that HE might forgive me for the days I fizzle. I don't anticipate that they will be flawless but then I expect me to be perfect.... for them.... and for the Master.

My real fear is that they are viewing me each minute of every day. not that they are holding up for me to make a "mistake" however I suspect that they will see me when I do and they do. They see me when I'm frail. They see me when I lose it. They see me when I fall. they see me when I fall apart. they hear each statement I say and how I say it and when I say it. Sometimes they comfort me and some of the time they duplicate me (great and terrible). they see me when I am depleted and when I am overpowered. i am an open book to them. sometimes a too much of an open book.....

they additionally see me when I triumph. They see me solid. They see me endure. They see me fall and get right back up fall down once more. They see me on my best days and when I attempt my best. They see me when I implore and put God first. When I trust and when my confidence is put under serious scrutiny. They see me when I love and when I live my life in love. They see me when I put others first and when I place myself last. They see and feel my unconditional affection for them.

They see the true me as my authentic self. They see me through the eyes of children, crude and genuine, and see that I am a long way from immaculate yet I'm being perfected... one day at a time. That I walk consistently, not holier than thou, yet in and with Blessedness Himself. They see the Great Potter forming this dirt into something lovely. They see me put in the red hot heater (furnace) and being refined with trials and tests. They see my affection for the Jehovah and my craving to commend Him and for every one of us to be a true living follower of the Christ.

Joy is a choice, it is a decision that you make that come what may, you are determined to stay in the "secret hiding place of Jehovah." In that place no one can steal your joy, because in the joy abounds, it is what is all around you, in that place. No one can penetrate your inner sanctum or sanctuary. Preserve for yourself a space, for just you and God. As long as you live things are going to happen to you, be it good or bad, right or wrong. It will not end until you expire. So find joy in the fact that Jehovah only wants our highest good. What happens out of that scope that he has for us is because of our own sins and imperfections. The bible also says that unforeseen occurrences befalls us all. In other words we may well plan a pretty picnic but we cannot predict the weather.

In face of fear, a natural catastrophe, or genocide, happiness simply doesn't appear to be the right response. even if there could be sights of it all over the place, we expect that communicating delight could be deriding the disaster. In any case that is not so much the right response.

Indeed, endless individuals (counting myself) have encountered profound delight right amid-st disaster, and not simply in impression,.

despite of the catastrophe. You are happy in light of the fact that you are "heart-torn open," in this sudden state of openness there is a feeling of profound adoration and a level of passionate exposure that we don't generally lay open to one another. Being in such a space together, being so vulnerable, so associated with one another, so united over all contrasts, is in fact happy, in a smooth kind of way.

Keep in mind, "Life's tests shouldn't incapacitate you, but rather it should help you discover who you are." And running across who you are incorporates uncovering that you are all of your feelings, not only some of the feelings, but all of them encompassed, in every sense of the word.

Seven Reasons to Bring Joy Back into Your Life:
1. Joy is one of the fruitages of God's holy spirit. It is one of the most prized possession a person can have.

2. Joy flows from the same source as love and peace; it flows from your heart.

3. Would you want to deny your loved ones your love and your peace? Of course not. Then please, don't deny yourself your joy either.

4. Don't push or force it either. When sadness comes, allow your tears to flow. When joy comes, allow your smile to shine. That's how it is supposed to be. It's your nature; it's who you are. There a time to weep and a time to skip about (joy). Jesus said weep with those who weep and rejoice with those who are rejoicing. There is a time and place for everything. However, joy at the right time is oh so sweet.

5. Joy is power

6. Joy is within each and every one of us.

7. To have joy is your birthright

Would you want to deny your loved ones that light? Of course not. Then please, accept it for yourself as well. When it shines, you can see the path in front of you, even if just one step ahead.

One step at a time, toward light—isn't that a fine way to respond to tragedy?

The deep joy flowing within you is a healing force. Its warmth has the power to melt the inner paralysis. Its energy has the power to fuel your journey toward a life in alignment with your heart's desire.

Would you want to deny your loved ones that? Of course not. Then don't deny yourself the power of your joy either. Because your heart's true desire is to live, and to feel joy.

But how? After tragedy, how do you even open your heart and mind to joy?

In that spirit let me present to you 21 of the infinite numbers of ways in which you could bring joy back into life.

In any case, I invite you to look at all these ways as possibilities, nothing more. Ponder them for a while, and then find out which one you feel most drawn to.

21 Ways to Bring Joy into Your Life1. Spend time with children (there are children everywhere).

1. Plant some flowers in a garden, fruits or vegetables
2. Read a childrens' book to a child
3. Travel (any distance)
4. Do something surprising for someone (great or small)
5. Go swing at the park to bring back that childhood nostalgia
6. Go to an art gallery (if you're into art)
7. Go listen to jazz (or any music genre that is your favorite)
8. Spend quality time with people you love (children, spouse or family)

9. Smile at strangers you make eye contact with
10. Help someone do something
11. Learn something new
12. Walk barefoot outdoors
13. Be in nature
14. Write thank you notes (even to yourself)
15. Give someone a card (anything that will convey you care or fits the occasion.)
16. Listen to music and really feel it.
17. Go to a poetry set or if you prefer you can do a sports game)
18. Allow someone else to help you and show them your gratitude.
19. Find simple pleasures in life (chaste and clean)
20. Stay polished in your spiritual routine
21. Continuously thank GOD for giving you joy in abundance.

God is and always is Jehovah

The Prayer of Jabez

The Prayer of Jabez

What do we learn for the prayer of Jabez?

Come with me into the mind of Jabez through Adam Clark.

Adam Clarke says of him: "There are several things in the account of Jabez that are very instructive:

"1. He appears to have been a child brought into the world with great difficulty, at the risk of his own life and that of his mother. So much seems to be implied in, she bare him with sorrow, i.e., with peculiar sorrow and danger.

"2. To perpetuate the merciful interposition of God in her own and her son's behalf, she gave him a name that must have recalled to her and his remembrance the danger to which both their lives were exposed, and from which they could not have been extricated but by the especial help of God. She called name Jabez, etc.

"3. He was brought up in the fear of God; he was no idolater; he worshiped the God of Israel, and he showed the sincerity of his faith by frequent and earnest prayer.

"4. His prayer at once was both enlightened and pious. He had piety towards God, and therefore he trusted in him: he knew that he was the fountain of all good, and therefore he sought all necessaries both for body and soul from him. He prayed to the God of Israel.

"5. Both the matter and manner of his prayer were excellent. His heart was deeply impressed with its wants, and therefore he was earnest and fervent; O that thou wouldest bless me indeed; 'O that in blessing thou wouldest bless me!' Let me live under thy benediction! Do thou diligently and frequently bless me!

"6. He prays for the things necessary for the body as well as for the soul: And enlarge my coasts—grant me as much territory as may support my family. Let the means of living be adequate to the demands of life; let me have the necessaries, conveniences, and, as far as they may be safely entrusted with me, the comforts of life! O that thou wouldest enlarge my coasts!

"7. He is conscious that without the continual support of God he must fail; and therefore he prays to be upheld by his power: That thy hand might be with me! May I ever walk with thee, and ever feel the hand of thy power to support and cover me in all the trials, dangers, and difficulties of life; and the hand of thy providence to supply all my wants in reference to both worlds!

"8. He dreads both sin and suffering, and therefore prays against both: O that thou wouldest keep me from evil, that it may not grieve me! Sin and misery are in every step of the journey of life; keep me from sin, that I grieve thee not; and keep me from sin, that I render not myself miserable! We can never offend God without injuring ourselves, he that sins must suffer. Thorns and scorpions are everywhere in the way to perdition; and he that walks in it must be torn and stung. He alone is happy who walks in the ways of God. Keep me from evil, that it may not grieve me.

"9. Prayers that have a right aim will have a right answer—Jabez did not pray in vain, for God granted him that which he requested. He was continually blessed; his family was increased; the hand of God was upon him for good. He was saved from sin, and saved from the pangs and sufferings of a guilty conscience.

"10. If we take up the character and conduct of Jabez in the view given by the Chaldee, we shall not only see him as a pious and careful man, deeply interested in behalf of himself and his family, but we shall see him as a benevolent man, labouring for the welfare of others, and especially for the religious instruction of youth. He founded schools, in which the young and rising generation were taught useful knowledge, and especially the knowledge of God. He had disciples, which were divided into three classes who distinguished themselves by their fervour in the worship of God, by their docilityin obediently hearing and treasuring up the advices and instructions of their teachers, and by their deep piety to God in bringing forth the fruits of the Spirit. The spirit of prophecy, that of prayer and supplication, rested upon them.

"11. He did not do these things merely as duty he owed to God and his fellows, but from the abundance of a generous and loving heart. In his counsel he erected a school of disciples. God had blessed him with temporal things, and he secures their continuance by devoting them to his service; he honours God with his substance, and God honours him with his especial blessing and approbation.

"12. On these accounts he was more honourable than his brethren. He was of the same stock and the same lineage; he had neither nobility of birth, nor was distinguished by earthly titles; in all these respects he was on a level with his brethren: but God tells us that he was more honourable than them all; and why? because he prayed, because he served his Maker, and because he lived to do good among men; therefore he received the honour that cometh from God. Reader, imitate the conduct of this worthy Israelite, that thou mayest be a partaker of his blessings.'

**"The things added by the Targumist might have been derived from authentic tradition."

So declares Adam Clarke's Commentary on this passage

My Story

My Story

At this point and time this took place in my life I was a single divorced parent, with only two children. I remember stopping at Subway on the way home. I happened to have with me a coupon for a free footlong sandwich. It was at the end of my work-shift, I had skipped lunch to get through the day faster, as I often did. Upon approaching the line to order my food, a man who looked very abstract and not even real came to me and asked me for a dollar. I had only a dollar to my name, in fact it was the only dollar until my next pay period. So I reached inside of my pocket to give it to him and he immediately said "No, keep it and put it in your Bible at Galatians, the 6th Chapter and pray to God for a car. He will answer you because you have found favor in his eyes." Now in amazement, I go to grab my food, catch the bus home and did just as he had mentioned. I prayed for a car, plus I took it an extra step and called a car dealership. By the time I was done, they told me to come in to sign the paperwork and pickup my vehicle. This was back in the late 90's. So I ventured off to the car lot and as promised by the mysterious man that begged for a dollar, I was the proud owner of a brand new car. For the fact that you did it for the least ones of these, you've done it or me! How true are these words. As I have often mentioned throughout this book, what you do for others, you ultimately do for yourself. I know that God doesn't need my money, but the fact that I was willing to give my last, to someone who was a stranger, moved things into my favor. I know that there are some of you that would think that this was just a coincidence. Well I say to you coincidence or not, it still worked in my favor.

I remember this story like it was yesterday. I had just came out of a nasty divorce from a man that was a perpetual liar and a cheat. If that wasn't enough, he wasn't the best father for my children neither. I had to depend completely on God. There was no other option. I had prayed to time immemorial for a vehicle., to no avail it never appeared. Then one day, out of the blue comes the unkempt man, who begs me for a dollar, my only dollar. It just goes to show you that the seeds that you sow can also produce expeditiously. There are many cases like this. There is no limit of how God may cause to act in our behalf. How will you know if your not in action?

Now, lets fast forward to 2013, when I started to write this book. I contracted MRSA Methicillin Resistant Staphylococcus Aureus. I went to Africa to join my new husband, in order to prepare for his visa. We were separated due to immigration laws and it took a toll on us both. So I flew there on July 31, 2013. About a week or so of being back on the fertile soil of Ghana, my husband noticed a bump on my right buttocks. He had reasoned it was probably hormones being released from our lost of our pregnancy with our daughter. Well, one evening, I had notice that the area was very itchy and had became inflamed. It got to the point were I could hardly get up to go to the restroom because of the intense swelling and pain. The swelling grew rapidly by the day, to eventually I couldn't walk to the restroom on my on. So my husband climbed a Neem tree and bathed me down in fresh medicinals oils that was released from rubbing them on the infection site. To no avail, it did not help not one iota. So he went to buy a blue salve from a medicine lady & used shea butter and bread to try to draw out the infection. It also did not help.

So as the days progressed, well my body started to shut down after 35 days of trying to fight this horrible flesh eating disease off. I started to give up and prayed to die, because death at the time looked more promising than life. Then my husband looked at me and said "You are not leaving me, I can't become a widower! I'm too young. Furthermore, I can't ship back a dead corpse of my wife home to my children!" I cried because then I started to feel guilty about how this would look. People would think that I traveled oversees and my husband murdered me. Then how my children would loose their mother and my youngest was only three and I had just stopped nursing him. This would have been hard on everyone. Especially my family who had not even the opportunity to meet my husband in person.

With much pressure my husband took out ten cloves of garlic and crushed it up on a spoon and begin to make me swallow them in spoonfuls while chasing it down with water. From each day forward that was my routine along with P-mar a Chinese doctor left behind. Each time I took it I would sweat for hours on end. I would get cold chills and shiver. He would also make me drink two young coconuts a day, and put me on a completely raw diet. Next, the greatest thing that was ever done to help aid my healing was Tea Tree oil. With prayer and affirmations it was healed. In December, right after my recovery, two weeks later, I was hit with breast cancer. We continued my regimen adding now raw juicing as well. My mother-in-law and sister-in-law told us where we could go to get some local spices. These spices were not your ordinary spices. Although the local women cooked with it, together with wasp spit and water I was blessed with this wonderful healing paste that healed my breast in 2 weeks exactly. The cancer came out in clumps and left two holes in my right breast. However, I am not complaining only relating how thoughts are powerful. I came across some research on how not forgiving yourself can be the culprit for why breast cancer develops. You may not agree with me on this, but whether it's true or not, since I've changed my thoughts, I've completely healed from it. I am still commanding my thoughts and no longer living on autopilot. I have possession over my own mind. I don't go to sleep worried anymore. I have gathered a wealth of information, I was compelled to share it. The best thing that ever happened to me is when I had no choice but to rely completely on the Creator. I have seen so many people out of fear run to the orthodox doctor to get cauterized, radiated, get organs burned up and hair fall out, bones break and get fractured, all in the name of being cured, but the reality of being cured escapes them. When in reality you are the cure! Yes I said it! You are the only one that has the power to heal yourself. Through God's healing power through foods and herbs. Although my story is not your story, God is Universal and the same healing power he used to heal me is still available. You can never exhaust his power. It has always been and always is., but don't take my word for it. Try him for yourself, I did! He has never ceased to amaze me! You see we need to stop looking at God like as if he's a man. He is a dynamic force, full of power and all the power there is or ever will be, he supplies. Stop looking for miracles, when you are one! Look inside you, look at you! His creation speaks about him and praises him everyday, he has unlimited advertising. My life is not the same. I was brought low so I can feel comfortable when the time came to rise up and soar high. Rise up I did indeed. Like the Phoenix I had a new birth of self awareness, a new outlook on life and God's purpose for me. This grounded me, and rooted me. I now have a deeper and more profound understanding, with intense appreciation for God.

I can't brag and say that I am God's poster child. However, I can say that I thought I knew him before, but I really know him now & he was nothing like anyone has ever described him to be to me. He is a all consuming fire and yet so gentle at the same time. I am his daughter. His tender mercy and undeserved kindness follows me all day long. I am more at peace with life and I feel his presence ever near me. Closer than hand & foot, more nearer, than the air that consumes me. In closing I encourage you to keep praying without ceasing. Constantly affirm your own good in this life. Yes, it's your birthright!

Be on the alert *qui vive** Do not deny which you are affirming and neutralize your good. Any time that you may feel like you swerving off course say "It is mines now" or as my adopted mother Beth would say "It's coming!" Whether it's, health, wealth, love, spirituality, pregnancy, job, happiness, abundance etc, never loose sight of the good that is in store, for those that are willing to put forth the effort. It is good with me now and always will be with the help of Jehovah. No other person compares to HIM. I am truly in constant amazement, because I was on my death bed twice and he answered my call both times. You don't have to go through what I went through in order to know that the seeds that you sow you are sowing for a lifetime. Once planted in the soil of your mind, unless uprooted will forever remain, good, bad or indifferent. So please, I ask that you walk away sowing good seeds, as much as you can find it humanly possible. Be the watchman over your thoughts and see how your life will expand with greatness and abundance adorns all around you and everything that you've been endowed with!

> **I pray that you be blessed all of your days. Commune with Jehovah, stay in prayer the whole day. Walk in Spirit, forever be grateful and thankful. It shall be well with you, in all that you do. My love for you comes from a higher place. May HIS love fill your life and fondle your soul.**

> **Dr. Nikki Krampah, CNHP, ND**

THOUGHTS ARE THINGS

You can never tell what your thoughts will do
In bringing you hate or love,
For thoughts are things, and their airy wings
Are swift as a carrier dove.
They follow the law of the universe -
Each thing must create its kind -
And they speed o'er the track to bring you back
Whatever went out from your mind.

-Ella Wheeler Wilcox

Printed in the United States
By Bookmasters